Tales of a
Ludicrous Bird Gardener

TALES OF A LUDICROUS BIRD *Gardener*

BILL ODDIE
OBE

Contents

Laura and I with a honeymoon souvenir.

Introduction

There is no shortage of books about how to attract wildlife to your garden. In recent years the category has almost caught up with self-help, cookery, dieting, and 'bucket list' books suggesting 50 thrilling things to do before you die. Believe me, in my case, reading a book won't be one of them. However, creating a wildlife garden might well be one of your intended gifts to posterity and what a splendid bequest that would be. However, beware of wasting the valuable time you have left dithering over which instruction book is the best. Their titles won't give you a clue because they are almost identical. Go to Google (or even pop in a bookshop) and you'll find *Gardening for Wildlife, Wildlife Gardening, How to make a Wildlife Garden, Creating a Wildlife Garden, All About Garden Wildlife, A Gardener's Wild Guide* and – the snappiest title of them all – *A Gardeners Guide to wildlife and birds and how to attract them.* That was just one Google page worth. I clicked my way to page 24 and found the list still going, albeit by then most of them referred to America. I imagine that, had I carried on, they would have more or less covered the world. This proliferation of information may appear to indicate that – as well as geographical variations – there are many differing approaches to wildlife gardening. But there aren't. At the risk of slightly offending authors (many of whom are, or were, my friends) I can reveal that although the titles may differ – a bit – the contents are almost identical. One might wonder why publishers keep commissioning the same book, but they do. You may also wonder why I have written another one, but I haven't. What would be the point? Let's face it, if people don't know by now how to create a wildlife garden, how to feed birds, make their own nest boxes, dig a pond and plant aquatics and bee-friendly flowers, they never will.

However, I am certainly not disparaging the instruction books that have gone before, or those currently in print, or ones which will appear in the future, I am simply assuring you that this is not another one. Neither is it a book about gardening.

It is however a book about gardens. *My* gardens. The ones I have known or owned during my life, from my toddling time to the venerable age I am now and hopefully will continue to be for a few more years. It is about memories, merriment and mishaps, many of them borne by the fact that I have never really known what I am doing horticulturally. I am untouched by Titchmarsh, Don or Dimmock. I do not subscribe to any gardening magazines, I am utterly ignorant of soil types, and I rarely even read the little labels on the plants that I buy, which no doubt explains why some of them don't survive. Neither am I concerned with tidiness, neatness or symmetry. In my opinion straight lines do not belong in a garden. It will not surprise you to learn that I am no friend of decking or paving stones. Crazy paving I don't mind. In fact, the crazier the better.

Being above all a lifelong lover of wildlife, I would consider a garden that has been allowed to become overgrown with weeds, nettles and brambles to be almost beyond improvement. My present garden has a few bits like that but is by no means unkempt. Indeed, it is more kempt than it may at first appear. I confess to being addicted to a style that some might call weird, others have called random, and I would call imaginative and creative. My wife came up with another word. One morning she was lured out onto the back lawn by a particularly delightful burst of British sunshine. This in itself surprised me. Not the sunshine, but the fact that my wife had strayed into territory she had avoided for several years. What she was now seeing was clearly affecting her emotionally, but was she impressed or was she disdainful?

I was curious, so I uttered a quizzical 'Yes? So?'

She fixed me with an accusatory glare and announced, 'This garden is ludicrous!'

I thanked her. Her pronouncement was clearly at best critical and at worst downright insulting. I took it as a compliment.

'Ludicrous? Good word. That is exactly how I want it to be. But in a creative sort of way.' I effortlessly segued into a eulogy. 'This garden is my canvas, my playground, and my hobby. And by the way, in case you are wondering, it is home to lots and lots of wildlife.' At which moment, as if too proclaim solidarity, a Robin hopped onto the back of my garden chair and half a dozen screeching parakeets landed on the Silver Birch thus obliterating any possibility of further discussion.

Not that I would have taken any notice. In my head I was already singing an adaptation of a stirring anthem from *The Desert Song*: 'This garden is mine.'

My wife retreated muttering 'Ludicrous,' leaving me to carry on touching up the gnomes.

It strikes me that there in that incident you have a compacted collection of garden-related experiences. It isn't just about planting, pruning and mowing. It is about disagreements, relationships, attitudes and complaints. It is about my neighbours, who hate the parakeets as much as I hate their cats. It is about the property developer who has bought the house on the other side and totally gutted the existing garden, which featured a small swimming pool, a model railway track and giant flagpole. This was admittedly strange, but surely more characterful than a square of what looks like astroturf hemmed in by tall grey fencing, thus creating an effect that has all the charm of a prison yard. And another thing. How come my wife, Laura, casts aspersions on my world of gnomes, fake animals and peculiar tableaux when her office shelves bulge with books of fantasy and legend, her job is writing for children's TV, and her hobbies include cutting windows in the cover of antique books to create a stage which she then populates with miniature figures, often indulging in somewhat dubious activities. Now some might call *that* ludicrous. I call it imaginative. She calls it art. More food for thought, all planted and grown in my little garden.

For the moment then, I shall call this book a history – a history of my gardens. A history of their wildlife, and of my life. From a muddy backyard in Rochdale just after the war, to an unkempt tangle in suburban

Birmingham during my teenage years, to a kid's trampoline-sized patio in Hampstead, to the ever-changing almost psychedelic ludicrous kaleidoscope that has been a godsend, a life-saver and an obsession for the past 25 years.

So, this book is not so much a 'How to ...' as a 'When?' and 'Why?'

Ah Yes, I Remember It ... Well?

We don't all have the same degree of sensory memories. What I mean is, some people have a strong emotive reaction to smells, others to sounds and others largely to visuals. Obviously some people have all three in equal measure, but lots of us are deficient in one or even two. It can be unnerving, but then it can also be a relief. An ability to forget is maybe every bit as vital as an ability to remember. I myself am particularly feeble in the nostalgic smells department and indeed there have been occasions on which I have been made to feel envious or even inadequate.

I feel positively deprived when anyone catches a whiff of a woman's perfume and exclaims almost ecstatically, 'That's the one my mother used to wear. I used to love it when she cuddled me to her breast, and it was like nuzzling into a beautiful scented flower. Even now, if a lady walks by wearing it she is in danger of being hugged, or even suckled.' At which point, I recognise that my so-called friend is teasing me, nay hurting me, by reminding me that in my childhood I had neither a sense of smell nor a mother. Actually, if all my friends were as mean as that I probably didn't have many of them either. Other homely aromas that I have been immune to all my life include freshly baked bread, the tang of crisp white sheets, and the fragrance of a newly mown lawn.

The fact is that I know not the frisson of any days gone by triggered by smell, but fortunately that doesn't mean I can't smell anything at all, as long as it isn't too far away. In order to sniff the whiff of spring blossom I have to risk getting a bee up my nose. A rose garden is not an entirely scentless zone, nor is chalk downland with the truly wild waft of thyme and other herbs that flourish there. As it happens, there are some aspects of natural history in which smell is of little significance to us. To many wild creatures, of course, it is of paramount importance, from mammals sprainting to insects spreading pheromones for sex and acids for defence. Some humans can pick up those smells. I can't. However, I am fortunate that my main area of enthusiasm and expertise is birds. Suffice it to say that neither I, nor anyone else I know, has only to sniff the air to identify a species of bird. 'Mm, I think I can smell a Red-flanked Bluetail.' I admit that even my nostrils are not completely insensitive to the fetid stench of a seabird colony, but frankly it doesn't make me wretch, which it does some birdwatchers. Mind you, I have always taken great care to avoid being spat at by a Fulmar, at the advice of an eminent British seabird expert who warned me, 'If you get Fulmar oil on your clothes you may as well throw them away.'

The fact that I can't smell noxious fumes is both a plus and a minus. 'Can you smell gas?' is not a question to ask me. I can tell you right now

'No. I can't.' But that doesn't mean there isn't a leak. A similar 'No' is often my response to whatever is making people with me overact in the way that only smells can provoke.

'Oh God. What is that? Yuck yuck. Poo poo. What is that horrible pong? Bill, surely you can smell that?' Can I?

This is one of the few times in life that I am prone to lie. If I say 'No I can't smell anything,' I immediately become the target of a 'Whoever smelt it dealt it' attack. If my grandchildren are there it will continue relentlessly for the rest of the day. If it's a family car ride it is total agony involving more chanting, pretending to vomit and opening and closing windows. So what do I do? I lie. I say 'Yes, it was me.' It would be nice to think that they are impressed by my confession, even though I must know I will be ridiculed. Not a bad lesson for life. But in fact they now let it drop, to coin a phrase, as if my confession has completely ruined their chance for teasing and taunting. Honesty is no fun, even if it's a lie. They also know that if they break into a farting contest in the car it will be totally lost on me.

'Grandad has no sense of smell.'

'No, but I can hear and that's the funny part. So keep going.'

They need no encouragement.

Born Not To Be Wild

Returning to memories of long ago, and I mean long long ago, I was born in 1941. A war baby no less. I wasn't aware of any smells of war, save perhaps the stifling rubbery sensation when you tried on your gas mask. This was long before I realised that I couldn't smell gas anyway. Actually that was more of an anti smell because it was almost impossible to breathe when wearing a gas mask. I suppose that was the idea but it was a tough choice. 'Which do you prefer? Poisoning or suffocation?' Happily I succumbed to neither, or at least if I did I don't remember about it.

Even though it was a very long time ago I do have a degree of aural recall of my young life in the early 1940s. The most vivid memory was the sound of the voices on the radio. This was known to us of course as the 'wireless,' which was perverse indeed since it clearly wouldn't work without a wire, and a plug and an electric socket, although that could be rendered useless during a power cut. Thus in a black out – ominous enough in itself – we were also deprived of music or various BBC voices. Otherwise, as soon as the electricity was back on, so was the wireless. In fact the wireless was never off. Never. Whenever and wherever I was in the house I could always hear it. It did not comfort me, it unnerved me. I couldn't decipher nor indeed understand most of the words, but I sensed that it spoke of doom, danger and deaths. 'Casualties' was the approved euphemism and still is. I probably heard Lord Haw Haw and Winnie Churchill and possibly I recognised moments of defiance, optimism or escapism, such as Vera Lynn singing 'The White Cliffs of Dover,' or Rochdale's very own Gracie Fields – 'Our Gracie' – before she abandoned 'Sally in our Alley' and sailed off to the 'Isle of Capri.' I daresay these forces sweethearts – Anne Shelton was the one my dad took a shine to – brought a degree of motherly comfort to a toddler. Nevertheless, to this day the sound of talk radio permanently on in another room still makes me feel anxious and afraid. I have cultured friends who ask me why I don't listen to Radio 4. I have a two-part answer. One, it reminds me of the war. And two, I don't understand a word of it.

Of course, my fear of war noises in the early 1940s was entirely justified. The nights were rarely silent. The wail of the air-raid siren was the most unnerving sound, followed by the ominous rumble of German bombers or the higher-pitched whine of smaller planes. Dad would comfort me: 'It's alright Bill, it's one of ours.' I believed him, but I am not sure he did. We were lucky to escape any war damage, which was especially fortuitous considering that our house was only a short way from the prime target of Manchester. We lived in Rochdale, which has now more or less merged into the nearby city and been incorporated into Greater Manchester. Had it been that way during the war I doubt that the enemy would have bothered to make any distinction. Having survived with its magnificent town hall unscathed, and our Gracie top of the pops, Rochdale by the mid-1940s had quite a noble and even romantic image. Alas, in more recent times it has become tainted by some appallingly perverse scandals, and the unsavoury reputation and grotesque personality of Cyril Smith. It is doubly sad because, as the city elders would surely remind us, the town has quite a reputation for producing generally cheery, clean-living and creative people, including Gracie Fields, Norman Evans, Mike Harding, Jane Horrocks and, dare I say it, even me.

Of course back in the early 1940s I knew nothing of this. It was revisiting my long-unvisited hometown for the very first edition of the still-thriving BBC series *Who Do You Think You Are?* that revived my mainly visual memories. What I had never realised during my early childhood was that I lived only a few miles from the stunning scenery of the lower Pennines. It was probably even more delightful back then, but we had no way of getting to it. My dad didn't have a car, I didn't have a bike, and I don't even remember going on a bus, except once to Belle Vue Zoo. The only thing I remember about that was the Big Dipper, which was a ride, not a bird.

The Taming of the Sparth

I did have a garden in Rochdale. Sort of. Almost. Well okay, a backyard. A very small backyard. Fortunately, although my senses of smell and hearing are poor, my visual recall is extremely vivid. I am fortunate to have what might almost qualify as a photographic memory. For example, if I am asked about a certain rare bird I found even 30 or 40 years ago, I can close my eyes and see the scene and in particular the bird, not just floating in some kind of vision but scuttling through the grass, wading on the shore, or perching on a dry stone wall just as it was when I first saw it all those years ago. I can enjoy edited highlights of my birding life without the hard work. At this very moment I can close my eyes and see a row of small houses with a sign saying St Albans Terrace, which is the kind of road name that could have been found in any part of the country. However, alongside it is another road sign that could surely only be found in a northern town such as say Rochdale. Sparth Bottoms Road!

Strangely, it is only when writing this book that it struck me that I had no idea exactly what a sparth is and whether or not it had a bottom. It sounds rather like some mythical monster. Or am I thinking of a snark? Maybe, but the true meaning is almost as fanciful. The only definition of a sparth I can find anywhere is that it is an obsolete Anglo-Saxon word for a battle-axe. As if to confirm its authenticity Chaucer writes: 'He hath a sparth of twenty pounds weight.' Chaucer does not make mention of bottoms, twenty pounds weight or otherwise. What Google also led me to was a splendid website called 'Sparth now and then,' which is brimming with sepia-tinted photos – some of places that I recognised – and recorded reminiscences in broad Lancashire accents which I thought I did recognise because they were exactly what I grew up with. What's more these archives reminded me of the chores we kids had to do, such as collecting the family coke. Coke was the low-grade waste product of coal, which literally fell off the back of a lorry. Collecting it involved trundling an old pram over the cobbles down to the gas works, past workers looking like characters from a Lowry painting. Everyone looked pretty much identical. Men in clogs, waistcoats and flat caps and women in aprons and headscarves. I felt I knew their names but of course I didn't.

The other thing I didn't know then was that my home patch in Rochdale was – and still is – known as Sparth. Sparth Bottoms Road runs from the highest point locally down to the bottom of the hill, which was no doubt considered the town centre because it housed the cotton mill, the gas works and the cricket ground with a rather smart white pavilion. In my mind's eye I can see them all. The only notable building at the top end of Sparth Bottoms Road – where we lived – was St Albans Church and the attendant graveyard. Even back then it was in some state of dilapidation with several gravestones keeled over and neglected, and what to us looked like concrete coffins with broken lids, or in some cases with sides completely missing. This was of course a great place for kids to play, or rather to scare the living daylights out of one another. Teasing lead to taunting and terrifying, which was enjoyed immensely by the perpetrators and dreaded by the victims. I was usually a victim.

Inevitably the favourite game was hide-and-seek. For some reason I seemed to do more than my fair share of closing my eyes and counting to 50 before I set off seeking the other boys who were hiding round the cemetery. The ones who were as chicken as I tended to hide ineffectively behind the graves so they were quickly found. As opposed to the bold ones who hid inside the graves.

It takes a special nonchalance not to feel genuinely edgy standing alone in a derelict graveyard when it has gone pitch dark and is totally quiet, and just as you are about to 'give in' in a Bunter-like way: 'Oh I say you fellows. A chap might be finding this a bit scary. Oh crikey!'

My excellent and much-admired Billy Bunter impression usually got a laugh, but not this time. There was total silence for what felt like half an hour, but in fact was probably two minutes, before one of my friends leapt out of a concrete coffin making banshee noises. I admit I screamed. Naturally I congratulated him on his hiding and timing, and then suggested that we went home. At which point he tapped me on the shoulder and whispered ominously, 'Bill … look.' He pointed me back towards the graveyard but I could see nothing new. Then, as we hurried on our way out, he grabbed my arm.

'There! There!' This time I saw something. Something moving inside one of the graves which was missing most of one wall. For a moment a white arm and hand appeared and gripped the sides. Then disappeared inside. Then it happened again.

'What is that?' I asked.

'Dunno, let's go and see.'

I declined, turned and exited, rapidly pursued by chicken noises. Not only did I not go and see, but I never, ever again crossed Sparth Bottoms Road, nor visited St Albans Churchyard, either to play or pray.

Of course I accept that this was all a schoolboy jape amplified by my timid little mind, but I will tell you this. I refer back to that excellent Sparth website. It records that in 1973 St Albans was totally demolished. Contemporary kids, and maybe some adults, were said to be relieved since they were scared to go there due to 'tales of the mad vicar.' I myself cannot help but be reminded of the chilling denouement of the movie *Poltergeist*: 'They only moved the gravestones.' I am not for one minute insinuating that Rochdale Town Council would have been so devious, even back in the increasingly decadent 1970s. Certainly if their website is anything to go by, the present residents of the area are proud to be Sparthans. Indeed so am I. Well I was for a while.

Pets and the Garden of Death

Like all kids of the immediate post-war era I spent almost 100 per cent of my leisure time 'playing out.' I am not going to join in the argument about whether or not children were healthier in them days, but lets face it there wasn't much to do indoors. There was still the wireless but that didn't keep me amused for more than the half-hour it took to get through *ITMA* (*It's That Man Again* with Tommy Handley). And surely parental concern about being careful crossing the road or taking sweets from strange men paled beside the constant fear of your sons or daughters being blown up by German war planes.

In essence I could wander wherever I wanted, and if I went missing no one in my family could go searching. My dad was at work, my mum was in hospital, and my gran – as far as I can recall – never went outside. Not that I was a great explorer. St Albans Cemetery was clearly cursed by zombies, so that was out. There was a fairly large wood down at the end of the terrace. It looked sinister, especially since there were very few leaves on the huge stark black branches. They had no doubt been denuded by acid rain and other pollution from the nearby factories and gasworks. If only to prove my schoolboy bravery, I felt compelled to clamber over the spikey iron railings, but was dissuaded by another boy – probably the fiend of the graveyard – warning me that there were dangerous animals in there, notably lions and tigers. Needless to say, my knowledge of species' geographical distributions was not as complete then as it became in later years. 'Blimey, man-eating carnivores down the end of our road?' I believed him.

So that was two natural playgrounds out of bounds. The place I did feel safe was the cricket pitch. Not the real proper grown-ups' gentlemen's club cricket pitch down by t' mill, but a grassless strip that ran along the back of our terraced houses. The condition of the wicket depended on recent weather and varied from dust to mud. Whatever the surface, it was scattered with stones and house bricks left over from the latest gang warfare. This was the scene of some of my most alarming early memories. Two gangs of small boys, none of them older than six or seven, standing face to face and pelting one another with extremely hard and dangerous objects. Eventually one gang would run away, but we knew that they would be back, especially if it was late autumn and we had started building our bonfire.

Basically the aim of the 'game' was to nick all the other gang's wood. If they made a successful raid, we were honour-bound to try and steal it back, and vice versa. As recorded by the excellent website our gang was called The Sparths – in this context battle-axes became more appropriate – and our deadly rivals were The Chaddies.

One of my final and most vivid memories of living in Rochdale was the winter of 1947. I was not much over six and not, as they say, 'a big lad.' Nevertheless, I swear that the snowdrifts at the back of our house were so deep that if, or rather when, I fell in I would disappear altogether. Once the snow was frozen I could climb up the slope until I could almost touch the top of the huge icicles that hung from the guttering. If I managed to break one off it was like a crystal spear. Six feet long and as sharp as a javelin. I can only thank the Lord that we didn't arm ourselves with them for gang fights. Fortunately, we were all preoccupied with sledging on what we referred to as 'the death run,' which was a slope on a nearby piece of waste ground. It was so-named not because it demanded advanced tobogganing skills but because little boys on sledges had no control whatsoever and could be literally lethal.

Not being a reckless kid I tried to avoid being purposely crashed into by the rough boys, which made it ironic that I managed to crash by myself and break a wrist by getting one hand trapped under the sledge. Instead of sympathy I got pelted with snowballs.

It is of course a proven cliché that we remember things from our childhood as being much bigger than they were. I remembered the snowdrifts as six-feet high and lasting for three or four months. I remember the cricket pitch as being as wide as The Oval, the battlefield being as big as The Colosseum, and the death run as being at least 100 yards long and almost vertical. However, when it comes to remembering my back garden the rule is reversed. I remembered it as small. In reality it was even smaller. Strictly speaking it didn't really qualify as a garden at all. It was more of a backyard. A small backyard. Frankly, it didn't have many or indeed any of the things normally associated with a garden. Like grass, or plants, or flowers. It did however have a sink.

At this point I daresay that enterprising and recycling-minded gardeners will proclaim that an old-fashioned ton-weight porcelain sink can be put to better use in a garden than in a bathroom. I totally agree. I myself currently have three of them with a cunningly concocted soil mix that turns them into mini-habitats. One of them is a miniature chalk downland, featuring mainly wild herbs such as betony and thyme, the second continues the theme with knapweed and harebells, and the third is mainly a tiny fairyland, where miniature fairies, dwarves and pixies battle with lions, tigers and bears. And of course dragons. For the moment I will say no more, but this may give you a preview – or a warning – of what is to come in my present ludicrous garden.

Meanwhile, the sink in our Rochdale backyard held no such whimsy. Nor was it used to grow anything in. It wasn't empty, nor full of water that could have made it a rather splendid backyard aquarium in which a nature-loving schoolboy could have kept newts and tadpoles. But not me. It was not a sink full of water, or even earth. It was a sink full of mud. About the only creatures I could have kept in there were mudskippers and lugworms. A passing sandpiper might have dropped down for a few minutes in order to probe for lugworms but it would have found nothing. Not that I had any idea what a sandpiper was. A bird perhaps? It is possible that whoever owned the house before us had used the sink to grow their own runner beans or sweet peas, but neither my dad nor my granny had any inclination to continue this horticultural tradition. Consequently, neither did I.

So the 'garden' consisted of a tiny concreted square with an old sink in it. Along the back wall there was a row of three wooden cupboards or cubicles, which were collectively referred to as 't' coal sheds.' In fact number one was the outside toilet. And number two... ? Sorry, the middle one, held a bit of coal, but mainly our supply of coke. Two things I recall about coke. One was that it was tricky to shovel because it kept sliding off the spade, but fortunately two, if you used your fingers they wouldn't end up as black as if you handled coal, which would release coal dust that got everywhere, especially on little boys' faces. I am sure you've seen the photos. I also remember something called 'nutty slack' which was even muckier. So cubicles one and two were environments to be visited as rarely and briefly as possible. However, number three was much more intriguing. It contained the animal action.

Number three was also somewhere to dump stuff we didn't want but hadn't got round to throwing away – throwing away was a habit that people got out of during the war – plus gear that we might only use now and then. This included a home-made cricket bat and wickets (formerly milk crates), punctured footballs and so on. Let's face it, it was a junk room, dark and damp. Nevertheless, this was the home of the family menagerie, in other words my pets. Several pets went in, but not all of them came out, usually because I forgot that they were there and consequently their feeding routine was sporadic sometimes to the point of fatality. Looking back it strikes me as unfair that my dad's pets were accepted as a far more integral part of the family. For a start they were allowed to live inside the house, in the sitting room no less. They were birds, but they were not mine, they were definitely dad's. Their names were Peter and Paul, which I am sure is clue enough to tell you that they were budgies. One of them was 'natural' green, the other was unnatural sky blue. I couldn't even tell you which was which, but dad conversed with them, and of course never ever forgot to feed them. The fact is, I suspect, that far from sharing father's affection for Peter and Paul, I think I resented them. There were times when I felt that they got more attention than I did, but then again it was impossible to ignore them because they were so irritatingly and incessantly noisy. The subdued and cheery chatter of most normal budgies, Peter and Paul amplified to a level that made it impossible to carry on a conversation or to concentrate on listening to the radio or to enjoy Vera Lynn's latest release. In truth I had little interest in listening to either, but I still found Peter and Paul's relentless chattering to be unbearably intrusive. I used to tell granny that she was lucky to be deaf, which would have been distasteful, but of course she couldn't hear me say so. Nor could she hear the blasted budgies. Eventually, after the birds had obliterated the warning of an impending air raid, and ruined most of the second day's play in the test match, father finally came round to my way of thinking and got rid of them. I don't know how. To quote the beloved kids' rhyme 'Fly away Peter, fly away Paul,' I assume that's what they were encouraged to do. But as for 'Come back Peter, come back Paul,' they never did. Leaving our household to experience a new and unfamiliar sensation. Silence.

My initial instinct was that dad had banished the birds to the backyard menagerie where previous pets had lived and died. I yanked open the creaky door on the third shed that was no more livestock-friendly than the outside toilet or the coke stash, but there was no sign of Peter and Paul, or their cage. But the mouse cage was there and so were the white mice, although one of them was rather less lively than the other. To paraphrase Monty Python from 25 years later, it was clearly an ex-mouse. By that evening its companion had also shuffled off its mousey coil and they presumably went together to meet their maker.

I fear I may be conveying an image that does not behove a man who has eventually devoted his life to animal welfare and love of the natural world. Several celebrity naturalists I can think of tell tales of their childhoods spent rescuing birds of prey, or adopting foxes or badgers, or sleeping in bedrooms that doubled up as animal hospitals, surrounded by developing tadpoles and wintering cocoons. The only creature that ever entered my bedroom was a big white cat that scared the life out of me by leaping on my head in the middle of the night. It gave me a fright that surpassed that of the ghost of St Albans graveyard, as well as leaving me with lifelong felinophobia. I was so shocked that I literally threw Fluffy – or Snowball or whatever it was called – against the bedroom wall. My intention was worse than the result. As cats usually do, it fell on its feet and sauntered out disdainfully. Even so, as cats also tend to do, it kept coming back. They are so arrogant that they simply refuse to believe that not everyone thinks they are beautiful. Tell a cat you hate it and it will take that as an invitation to sit on your lap sharpening its claws on your kneecaps and start purring. At which point its owner will really annoy you by saying 'Oh, she likes you.' At which point you are perfectly entitled to throw the owner against the wall as well.

Such an exchange never happened between my father and I but the facts were clear. We soon negotiated the age-old bargain between parents and child. The cat was dad's — and he was welcome to it — but I would be allowed a pet of my own as long as I was sure that I could look after it myself. I chose a tortoise. There was no reason to doubt that it was perfectly happy in the backyard, although be honest it isn't easy to be sure if a tortoise is happy or not. They don't wag their tails, they don't purr and they don't roll over so you can tickle their tummy. You can of course put them upside-down and if you do tickle them they are likely to wave their legs around, which may denote happiness, or even laughter, but is more likely panic. If you want to play pussycats with a tortoise you can hold them in your lap and stroke them, but who knows if they feel anything?

I may have been given my tortoise as a birthday present in July. Throughout the summer and early autumn I proved myself to be a natural born tortoise-whisperer. I didn't have to take him for walks, but I did occasionally shift him around the yard so that he got some exercise. Now and then I put him on or in the sink full of mud and chucked him a handful of rejected salad or vegetables so that he could pretend it was his very own dining table. It was disconcerting when one evening I found him on his back, presumably having lumbered to the edge of the sink, fallen off and gone topsy-turvy. We didn't risk it again. From then on he dined on the floor, which made feeding time even easier as all I had to do was open the back door and chuck out a handful of soggy greens.

It wasn't the seminal relationship that turned me on to nature, but at least I did learn a few basic facts. One of them was that some animals hibernate and that tortoises are among them, and that included mine. I suspect that I got a bit of instruction from 'nature time' at my primary school, when kids were allowed to bring in their pets — well the ones that the teacher approved of – and they could ask questions about looking after them. I took in my tortoise shortly before Christmas. Throughout the lesson he remained motionless in his shell. The teacher suggested that perhaps by now he should be in hibernation, whilst an unkind boy suggested that he already was. Or worse. I swore I could sense movement and the teacher backed me up. He may have just been protecting my feelings but in any case he allowed me to pop tortoise back in his box and I was allowed to go home early with instructions to commence the hibernation procedure as soon as possible.

The official tortoise winter quarters would be outside the house but not exposed to the elements. Thus where white mice had once scampered and died, my tortoise would now sleep. I had somehow acquired a tea chest. I filled it with lots of straw, then I placed my pet on his cosy bed and added a few more layers of straw on top so that he was totally incarcerated in warmth and protected from the bitter months that constituted what went down in the record books as one of the worst winters ever. Temperatures remained around zero and below for months and months. My tortoise snoozed on, or at least I assumed he did. I knew not to disturb him, so I didn't. In fact, I'll be honest, I forgot that he was there. I remembered some time in May. One of the few olfactory memories I do have is the smell of rotting tortoise and I hope it is a smell I never experience again. Before I lifted his straw blanket I willed him to be having the tortoise equivalent of having a bit of a lie in. Two or three months' worth. But my nose was telling me the truth. As I gingerly removed more straw I had to accept that I was guilty of criminal negligence. If not tortoisecide. I have blanked what happened next but

I suspect that I carried him across the yard, probably on the coke shovel – tortoise corpses tend to be less messy than other animals because their innards are contained in their shells – and I buried him in the sink.

The truth is that at the age of six the part played by animals and birds in my life was minimal. Indeed livestock had reason to regard me as a liability or a threat. Then one day something happened which literally changed my life. What's more it happened in our garden. Our front garden.

One Flew Into the
Dunnock's Nest

I know I said that St Albans Terrace didn't have front gardens and strictly
speaking this is true. However, what we did have was a dense privet
hedge that ran parallel to the houses alongside a narrow path past the
front doors. Some doorsteps might have a little plant pot next to the milk
bottles but there was no space for any large plants or shrubs. In effect then,
our front garden was a couple of yards of thick privet hedge bordered
on either side by more privet hedge leading down the hill to the cotton
mill and up the hill to the main Manchester Road. It was hardly an ideal
garden for playing, but I tried. One day I was kicking a ball or a tin can, or
was it a brick, and it rolled underneath the hedge, disappearing amongst
the dead leaves, cigarette packets and beer bottles that were littering the
earth and rubble. It is very dark inside a privet hedge so I had to crawl on

my hands and knees, lacerating my legs on broken glass and my cheeks on broken branches. As I rummaged with the typical determination of a schoolboy wanting his ball back I began to sense that I was being watched. I looked up. Something looked down. A pair of shiny little eyes peeping over the lip of a mossy little nest. I learnt later that the eyes and nest belonged to a Dunnock, or Hedge Sparrow as it was known back then. All I knew was that it was a bird and, since it was sitting tight rather than flitting away, chances are that it was sitting on eggs.

Generally speaking the young schoolboys of today know that it is wrong to scare a bird off its nest, and even more wrong to handle the eggs, and unforgivably wrong to take one home, and an act of juvenile delinquency to own an egg collection. Such is the admirable morality as taught by the likes of the RSPB and *Springwatch*. But in my childhood there was no *Springwatch*. There wasn't even a telly. The only nature club I belonged to was the 'I-Spy' books in which you ticked off sightings until you had earned a notched feather. Which let's face it in itself doesn't sound entirely appropriate. I sometimes wondered what species the scarlet or purple feathers had come from. Just as I was wondering what had laid the eggs in the little nest and what colour they were.

This is a story I have told before but it remains unique so forgive me if I tell it again. Quickly. Three of the eggs were greenish-blue. The fourth one was whitish with brown blotches. The only Cuckoo's egg I have ever found in the whole of my life. I took it, wrapped it in my hanky, climbed over the backyard wall and squashed it. When I finally realised that it would have been something of a star item in a schoolboy's egg collection I was quite upset. Although I took small consolation from someone pointing out that by taking and breaking that egg I had saved the lives of three young Dunnocks, although I didn't come to look at it that way for several years.

Meanwhile I suspect that my reputation was growing more notorious amongst the nesting birds of Sparth Bottoms Road, and possibly also with the neighbouring householders, the custodian of the churchyard and the keeper of the golf course. My dad received regular phone calls: 'Your boy's stuck up our apple tree. He were scrumping,' or 'He's wedged between the railings, trying to get at our conkers,' or 'He ran right across the green at the 18th just as our captain was going for a birdie. He made some daft joke about him going for a birdy too. A Skylark or summat. Once more and I call the coppers.'

My father once imparted this piece of wisdom to me: 'Bill, just because grown-ups are older doesn't mean they always know best.' Having said that, he was himself dignified, scrupulously law-abiding and probably did know best. He would understand and tolerate juvenile high jinx such as scrumping apples and brick frights, but trespassing and molesting wildlife would surely bring shame on the family, let alone putting the golf pro off his stroke. In Rochdale in 1947 this was not acceptable. Next spring we moved to Birmingham.

Oak Tree Crescent

In Rochdale our home had fitted right in, squeezed halfway along a terrace in which humble abodes were stacked together like a giant pack of cards. The rooms were very small and dark and the garden didn't deserve the name. However, our new house in Quinton, Birmingham, undoubtedly bore witness to the fact that dad had climbed a couple of rungs up the ladder of success at the Midlands Electricity Board. To be honest I had never been aware that dad was in electricity. I later discovered that his first job in Rochdale after leaving school at 14 was selling lightbulbs and presumably a few plugs and fuses. This must have been a challenge since it was during the war when light was generally discouraged. I am guessing but perhaps dad took an apprenticeship course in accountancy, although nightclasses can't have been easy during the blackouts. Anyway, I suspect that the outskirts of Birmingham were considered more salubrious than the middle of Rochdale and his new job of Assistant Chief Accountant more prestigious than whatever he was up t'north. Certainly Oak Tree Crescent sounded more attractive than Sparth Bottoms Road. The street was a cul–de–sac, which boded well for mornings more peaceful than the clogs chorus. The houses were semi-detached, had bay windows, front gardens and drives, and were appropriately leafy, not only with oak trees.

I was about six when we moved. The day we moved in I, and I daresay dad also, noted agreeable signs of healthy and non–violent youthful activities. There were wickets chalked on a garden wall, with a lamppost conveniently positioned for bowling from. Two small boys were hunched behind a hedge firing fake guns. Our house overlooked the turning circle at the far end of the road, which was our equivalent of The Oval. It was as safe and as peaceful as it could be. Moreover, compared to Rochdale the house was much bigger. So was the garden.

In fact we had two gardens, although the front one didn't really count. It was neat to the point of artificiality, being just a small square of grass. It had a pebble surround and about a metre of privet, just to remind me of Rochdale, not that I ever saw a bird in it during all the time that we lived there. No doubt the birds preferred the back garden if only because, instead of being neat like the front, it was a complete mess.

The centrepiece was a lawn which during the early years served pretty well as a venue for playing either football or cricket, along with one other little boy who lived next door. Until I made more friends, both sports were one to one rather than team games. The lawn, which was not exactly trim when we arrived, was most suited to a vastly simplified version of football sometimes referred to as 'three and in.' One striker against a goalkeeper. Score three times and you swap over. One might assume that kicking the ball might be more exhilarating than catching it, but in fact I much preferred being in goal. Diving and saving, especially off the ground, which felt almost like taking flight. The fact that you often ended up splayed flat out in the grass meant it felt only fair that the striker had to go and get the ball – whether he had scored or missed – especially if it flew over the fence into next door's garden, where there was danger of it landing on something fragile like a prize rose bush, a dog or a baby. Anyone who has been confined to a garden to play ball games will I am sure confirm that there is a limit to how many times you can call out 'Please can we have our ball back?' or have to go round and knock on the front door, or – most traumatic of all – get caught climbing over the fence. At which point the neighbour often resorted to confiscation: 'And you are not having it back.' Eventually both football and cricket became unsustainable as more and more balls got lost or confiscated and the pitch became less and less playable as seemingly overnight the grass on our lawn grew and grew and grew. The reason was simple enough – nobody cut it!

I should at this point quickly explain the Oddie family situation at the house in Oak Tree Crescent. I have often wondered what was written on the census form. There should've been a census in 1941 but there was a war going on so it was cancelled. In fact in 1941 I was being born, so I would have missed it anyway. So too did my mum and dad. Ten years went by until the census of 1951 which oddly I do remember, probably because I heard dad talking about it, maybe to me, or more likely to his mother, my granny, who lived with us. My mother didn't live with us. She never really had, and never did in the future. It is a story I have related in my autobiography, *One Flew Into the Cuckoo's Egg*, and on the telly in *Who Do You Think You Are?* The plain fact is that my mother was never a permanent resident at either Sparth Bottoms Road or Oak Tree Crescent. A lot of the time she was in a psychiatric hospital, and at other times she was… somewhere else. I do remember her making one or two appearances in Birmingham, including one occasion commemorated with a black-and-white snapshot of her lounging in a deckchair. She was near to if not literally in the garden. But she wasn't mowing the lawn.

Neither did dad. As far as I know he didn't have some kind of phobia or a conscientious objection to gardening, but I never saw him do it. Any of it. No weeding, no planting, no pruning, no growing and never ever any lawn mowing. He wasn't lazy, just apathetic, or preferred other pastimes such as darts, bowls and the occasional football match. In other words things that took him out of the house and away from his wife, who just might turn up and cause a scene, from me, who came and went collecting birds' eggs and playing rugby, football or cricket, and from granny, who was ever-present every minute of every day. Actually, I suspect that she was reason enough for dad to ration his time at home. I know that I myself resented the amount dad was dominated by gran. Her constantly intrusive presence made it hard for him to talk to me and, even more sadly, to his friends. He had plenty of workmates but he never invited them home. He clearly had no intention of ever doing so. There was no incentive to spruce up the house, refresh the sitting room furniture, and probably least of all do anything constructive in the garden. Like, for example, mowing the lawn. Thus the grass continued to grow.

Dad ignored it in protest. I thought that perhaps some day it could be considered a small nature reserve.

And granny? One afternoon I came back from school. Dad was still at work. Granny was nowhere to be seen – maybe she's asleep, I thought. I sauntered into the kitchen to get a dandelion and burdock. As I sipped it I gazed out of the kitchen window overlooking the lawn. The grass was now so long that it was easy to imagine a mahout on an elephant lumbering through it. Not that that was a sight I was familiar with at the age of 10. Nevertheless, I sensed that there was something strange going on. The grass was moving. Imperceptibly. Nothing visible, just the sign of its presence. Something prowling, creeping, maybe stalking. If I had been at Corbett National Park in the north of India my pulses would have been racing, my breath quickening and my emotions suspended between fear and anticipation. That's how I saw my first Tiger. As I watched it I thought 'you know, that's exactly like my granny in our garden.' Now that's something I never thought I would say: 'My granny was like a tiger!' But for one afternoon she was – crawling through the grass on her hands and knees, snipping away with a pair of kitchen scissors.

She said nothing, but her response and motive were obvious. She gave me a look – a glare – that said: 'You should be doing this. Not a frail old lady like me. And as for your father. No wonder he doesn't invite any of his friends back with a scruffy garden like this.'

I resisted the temptation to mutter 'Gran, he doesn't invite them back because you embarrass him.'

Then, with the sort of conclusive statement that people resort to when they wish to extract themselves from something they wish they had never started, she announced aggressively, 'Well, I am not doing it any more. If he wants a nice lawn he can do it himself.'

So saying, granny flopped down in the long grass and became invisible. I tracked her down and helped her to her feet, carefully relieving her of the scissors. If running with scissors is risky, crawling with them could be fatal. I led her to the deckchair, refraining from muttering: 'I know you are just trying to make him – and me – feel guilty, but dad doesn't care about the garden. And neither do I. Yet.' But I had plans.

I was a Juvenile Ringer

To coin a reference from a well-known black-and-white scary movie of the 1950s, 'I was a teenage birdwatcher.' Not that there was anything weird and spooky about that. However it was considered slightly abnormal behaviour for a young lad. I still threw myself frantically into appropriately boyish pursuits such as making model planes, stamp collecting and playing rugby, football and cricket on the local wasteground meadow, our lawn having been declared totally unplayable. I shared most of these pastimes with like-minded chums but I kept quiet about the birdwatching. At that time it was a secret and solitary pursuit that might have attracted suspicion and derision. Echoing Oscar Wilde, I used to think of it as 'The hobby that dare not speak its name.' For a fuller account of how I eventually came out and subsequently spread all over the place, I can only immodestly refer you to some of my own books such as *Gone Birding, Follow that Bird* and *Gripping Yarns.* In the early 1950s though,

I was largely the lone birdwatcher. I wandered the local farmland in search of nests and eggs, day after day I cycled to the bleak and often birdless Bartley Reservoir, and I rather prematurely got into bird ringing, which of course first involves bird trapping.

I can't believe that what I used to do was entirely legal. Certainly for as long as I can remember you have had to qualify for a licence to capture, handle and ring birds under the auspices of the BTO (British Trust for Ornithology). There was probably an age restriction for this. I don't know what it is or was but I am pretty sure that at 12 I was well under it. I have a vague memory of a periodic 'hobbies for boys' magazine which had an advert offering 'plastic colour rings and a free application tool.' The tool was little more than a small aluminium spoon with which you could slide the ring onto a bird's leg, rather as one would use a shoehorn on tight boots. This was obviously not part of any official scheme and the rings were not metal and were not inscribed with a number and an address to report to if the bird was found again, dead or alive. It used to be 'Inform BTO British Museum Nat Hist London SW7,' nowadays 'www.ring.ac' is the contact.

The plastic rings were featherweight which somehow comforted me, as well as the bird I presume, and they came in a variety of colours. This at least allows you to know if the same birds are resident, wandering or returning. It's called colour-ringing and the practice still goes on today – and it will probably continue until miniature digital geolocators take over completely. There is, however, one problem that I doubt will ever be a total doddle. In order to put anything on a bird's leg, you first have to catch it.

The Garden Ringing Station

I don't recall if the bootleg bird-ringing magazine sold traps, or whether I couldn't afford to buy one. In any event, at that stage in life I could rarely resist a challenge to 'do it myself' no matter how deficient I was in the necessary skills. It is a trait that continues to this day, much to my wife's exasperation. I always resist 'getting a man in' to do a job I can do myself, especially if it involves balancing on high ladders or fiddling with live electricity. She says she's only warning me for my own good, which at least it shows that she cares. I think. Anyway, I was utterly adamant that no hands, skilled or otherwise, would touch my traps. They were constructed out of 'chicken wire,' which I trimmed and bent into rectangular sections. A wire box, if you will. The front wall – the door – was attached by little loops like hinges. I then placed a saucer of water and a few seeds or crumbs inside the trap and propped open the front door with a stick. The basic principle was that a bird hopped in to get the food. The stick was whipped away and the hinged door would drop down shut, thus capturing the quarry. I soon discovered that if I remained within stick-yanking distance the birds wouldn't go in. What was needed was a length of stout string tied to the stick and stretching to a hiding place some yards away. From here an operator could pull the string, dislodge the stick, release the door and catch the bird. Our little bicycle shed was ideal cover. The ideal operator – in fact the only available operator – was granny.

I would like to think that despite having resigned herself to the fact that the lawn would never be the pristine bowling green she dreamed of, she nevertheless found consolation in being given such a responsible task as trap-triggerer. It was also her task to jot down the birds' measurements in the ringing log, something which is very tricky if your hands are filled with Great Tits and Song Thrushes (oh yes, there were plenty of Song Thrushes in them days). I thought of that garden – and still do – as my 'home ringing station.' Colour-ringing taught me that there were far more individuals visiting the garden than I had thought. My memory, however, assures me that there were far more birds everywhere then than there are nowadays, or is that an exaggeration through the rose-coloured spectacles of ageing? There were also almost permanently resident Hedgehogs, which resided in a broken lattice-frame at the bottom of the garden.

Interlude: The Travelling Trapper

The novelty and the rank inefficiency of the garden ringing station meant that its appeal began to pale. I am not sure if granny ever enjoyed it as much as I did and in any case I had finally investigated the rules and etiquette of proper BTO-type ringing. This took me on a truly seminal journey of delight and discovery at Monks' House Bird Observatory, which was on the Northumberland coast opposite the wondrous Farne Islands. In two weeks in spring I learnt so much, including the pain of pulling Puffins. The Puffins were pulled, but the pain was all mine when they lacerated my hands with their claws and tried to prune my fingers with a beak that resembled a pair of secateurs. Having seen a Puffin holding a dozen sand eels between its mandibles I am sure they could get a handful of fingers in there with no trouble. As it happens I was quite proud of my fingers in those days as I was often the only one dexterous enough to be able to extract Long-tailed Tits that were entangled in mist-nets. No bird gets tangled quicker than a Long-tailed Tit, nor has so many bits and pieces that can get totally wrapped up in the mesh. More than once I have witnessed a ringer's ultimate embarrassment when he triumphantly believes he has freed the bird, only to realise that it has left its tail behind. Even though I say it myself, I was quite an adept ringer, and frankly was not surprised when I passed my ringing test, got my licence, acquired my own nets, and obsessively set myself the challenge of ringing every Greenfinch in Bartley Green. Evening after evening I used to cycle the two or thee miles to where there was a gulley full of tangly hawthorns which held a Greenfinch roost for most of the year. No other species. No Chaffinches, no House Sparrows, just Greenfinches. Heaven knows how many I caught and ringed. Eventually I was informed that one of my birds had been found dead a few miles away near Bromsgrove. The fact that it was called a recovery seems cruelly ironic. A live bird is a retrap and I did retrap lots of my birds, which I suppose constituted a small contribution to ornithological data in that it proved that Bartley Greenfinches were largely sedentary. But of course it wasn't the science that lured me, it was the challenge to myself. One boy and his birds. All alone in the woods and then cycling back in pitch darkness. You wouldn't get the BTO encouraging kids to do that nowadays.

Going back to the house in Oak Tree Crescent was frankly something of a last resort. I spent far more time at school doing extracurricular activities, including all manner of sports, designing posters for 'societies' and eventually writing songs and sketches for the school revue. I sometimes cycled to school, which was nearly an hour's journey, although this was probably quicker than taking the two or three buses necessary to get from Quinton to Edgbaston. Having my bike meant that I could avoid going straight home after school and could maybe go via a couple of local reservoirs. During the school holidays I spent even less time at home. My cycle journeys got longer and my vigils at Bartley stretched literally from dawn to dusk. Inevitably, I haven't been able to resist writing about this period in my life. You can't write an autobiography without mentioning childhood. I have even had people express their sympathy as if I'd had a tough time, but I don't think I deserve that. Our home wasn't unhappy, it was just boring. Mum wasn't there. Granny always was. Dad worked long hours, often burning the midnight light bulb doing the company accounts. If he wasn't at work he'd be having a sedate pint and game of darts down The Stag and Three Horseshoes, which was about 20 minutes' walk from home. I knew I could always find him there if there was a crisis, like granny losing her false teeth. Or the afternoon I came home to find mum naked in the bath. As I recall, that totally surprise visit went quite placidly, and indeed that was the occasion mentioned previously when I even took a black-and-white snap with my Kodak Brownie of mother relaxing in a deckchair, looking content and surveying the garden. It was the one and only time the garden fulfilled its proper function. I wonder now, was mother happy, or was she thinking: 'By heck, that lawn could do with a good mow.'

It didn't get any better. Mum turned psychotic again and was sectioned and taken away. Granny lost interest and considerately passed away when I was on holiday with a friend in the Lake District. Dad, free of his mother's domination, played even more darts and bowls – well enough to win a couple of shiny cups – and had the front room decorated and kitted out with a new blue three-piece suite. He also bought a new-fangled record player with some old-fashioned records. For the first time in my life I saw him invite workmates to our house to have drinks and play cards. I believe he was actually proud of the house.

However, I daresay he was a bit ashamed of the garden. He probably blamed me. 'Bill wants it to be a bird reserve, so I can't do anything with it. Apparently its best for the birds if it's like that.'

'What? A total mess?' ribbed a friend and everyone laughed. Including dad who clearly had no intention of ever doing any gardening anywhere, ever.

For my part neglect was just fine. In truth I hardly thought of the garden as a nature reserve, but looking back now I appreciate that just letting a garden go wild is possibly the best way to attract wildlife. By the way, the best bird I saw there was a male Reed Bunting perched on what used to be the goalposts.

Time Passes

In the autumn of 1960 I went off to Cambridge University. I had a rather swish little room at Pembroke College, in what was then known as the New Block – it still is! My window overlooked a large lawn which was surrounded by flowerbeds clearly tended by someone who knew about proper gardening. It was pretty but it wasn't 'natural,' and of course it wasn't mine.

When I went back for the Christmas holiday I had to face the fact that 8 Oak Tree Crescent wasn't mine either. Dad had very sensibly sold the semi and bought a spacious and rather swish flat on a private estate in Hagley – a rather sumptuous area in Worcestershire which has probably now been absorbed into Birmingham's commuter belt. Maybe it was then. I know dad used to drive to the electricity board's new HQ in an almost flashy and unnecessarily large Ford Zephyr 6. It could do 102mph. I know that because I borrowed it to tazz down to Slimbridge on the recently opened M5. Two things – I hope he never knew, and I hope he never drove that fast.

At this time I was delighted that dad was at last enjoying some freedom and adventure, and most of all company. I suspect he even considered female company. Heaven knows I tried to matchmake him with his secretary. I even admitted that I now had a proper girlfriend. I don't know if I was challenging him or encouraging him, but it didn't work. I always felt that dad had a guilty streak in him that stopped him 'going for it,' as they say. Or maybe he had weathered such a long hard time coping with his wife and mother that he had resolved to avoid anything like that for the rest of his life.

Sadly, the rest of his life wasn't very long. After a lifetime of smoking like a chimney, coughing his lungs up, and gasping for his inhaler – all of which I painfully witnessed – he died two decades younger than I am now. I have never smoked since.

Living in the City

In 1964 I moved to London. Let's face it, it is not the tradition of students just down from uni to live anywhere that has its own garden. Some student flats are lucky to have a bedroom and a bed, but certainly not a flowerbed. Setting up a window box or buying a cheap houseplant are about as near as you are likely to get to gardening. Local bird life is most likely to be a pair of London pigeons that nest on the window sill, squit on the postman and keep you awake. You might try sticking one of those little plastic feeders on the window, but the cost of bird seed and peanuts would soon make a hole in your student grant. When times are hard you might resort to eating bird food yourself – some of it could pass for muesli. At least if you are above ground-floor level you might be able to look down from on high. Adjacent gardens are likely to be pretty much abandoned but you do stand a chance of spotting a family of urban foxes. They'll keep you awake too.

My first London abode was in Paddington, about 100 yards from the station (we didn't have metres in those days). It was a very busy area and frankly I couldn't even sense the presence of anything garden-ish. Fortunately, if I wanted greenery and ponds or even lakes it was only a short walk to Hyde Park. Which, as it happens, I don't remember visiting once. It seems to be only relatively recently that we have begun to appreciate that London's parks are well worth watching for wildlife. Nevertheless, that first flat had its memories. I shared with Stephen Frears, the now widely lauded film director whose works include *The Queen*, *High Fidelity*, *Philomena* and many more. At that time Stephen was directing a show at the Establishment Club in Soho – one of those seminal Sixties venues that launched a whole school of comedy featuring the likes of Peter Cook, Bird and Fortune, Lenny Bruce and Frankie Howerd. Music was provided by The Dudley Moore Trio plus various singers. It was a 'various singer' called Jean Hart who changed my life and, although I didn't appreciate it for many years, my attitude to gardens and gardening.

All I need tell you now is that after a year spent treading the boards in New Zealand, New York, and on tour across America along with the likes of John Cleese, Graham Chapman, Tim Brooke-Taylor and Willie Rushton, Jean and I got married and began the business of climbing the London property ladder. Maybe the fact that we never looked beyond an area of North London that featured such green oases as Regent's Park, Primrose Hill and Hampstead Heath meant that a garden was not our top priority. In fact I don't recall even discussing it. Over a relatively short period we started in a ground-floor flat in Belsize Park with a small square of a backyard which was so shaded that nothing could grow in it, not even grass. It made the Sparth Bottoms Road sink full of mud look like Versailles.

We stayed there long enough to have our first daughter, and then decided to move before we had another one, which we soon did, to a bijou little three-storey 'town house' (estate agent jargon for a house in town). It had a spacious basement sitting/dining room with adjacent galley kitchen, a ground floor lounge, a master bedroom, a second bedroom big enough to accommodate children's bunk beds, and an attic office which doubled up as a music room that held a permanent drum kit and a sparingly played tenor saxophone. Each room had a small south-facing window, which would have looked out onto a garden, had there been one. But there wasn't. The houses around there were so tightly packed that they almost touched one another. The back window had a close-up view of the brick wall of a recording studio. There was a narrow gap just big enough to accommodate a small flowering tree – maybe a magnolia – that I suspect Jean may have planted. It certainly wasn't me.

I liked that house. Many interesting people came by, mostly from the music world. Mainly Jean's lot. Miles Davis's then drummer Jack DeJohnette played my drums and rummaged through my records. We ended up reviewing new albums by the likes of The Band and Weather Report. Believe me, to an innocent mouth-organ player from Rochdale this was heaven. It was a pretty groovy atmosphere for our young daughters too. In my experience, little kids don't get kept awake by music, they sleep through it. If they didn't we could afford a 'mother's help' – who occasionally helped father a bit too – who used to wheel the girls across the road to the peace of Primrose Hill if they were being kept awake by a jam session.

So we all had plenty of fresh air and yet at some point someone, maybe both of us, maybe the kids as well, maybe even the mother's help, said: 'You know it would be really nice if we had a garden.' Nobody disagreed, but there was additional persuasion from my accountant. This was the mid-1970s and frankly I was doing rather well. *The Goodies* was regularly watched by over 10 million people, and whilst we weren't going to make fortunes from BBC fees alone, I had not inconsiderable additional income from having written all the music, including five top-twenty singles. I confess, I can imagine some serious songwriters who might resent the success of tracks such as 'The Funky Gibbon' and 'Black Pudding Bertha.' I could certainly understand it if they were envious of the rather special house I was able to buy. I don't recall how much I paid for it, but whatever it was in the 1970s wouldn't get you a garden shed these days. Not that we had a garden shed then, but we did have a garden.

The Ideal Home

I can readily recall the first time Jean and I viewed the house. It was fairly typical for North London, being at the end of a Victorian section of terrace which had mercifully been spared modernisation. The adjacent house was built entirely of grey concrete both outside and in, including the furniture. Ours was rather more traditional. We would have more rooms than in our previous house, indeed maybe too many. Jean declared that we could fix that by employing one of her art-school friends who now ran his own building company specialising in conversions. That's one of the possible advantages of being married more than once. You might change some of your friends, but you don't have to lose your plumber, electrician or builder. 'The Knockers Through' was a satirical sobriquet for middle class *nouveau riche* customising their houses in Hampstead, which I suppose is what we were. Downstairs, three smallish rooms became one spacious kitchen with sliding glass doors that led out to the garden and beyond. 'Beyond' was something of an understatement.

As we walked back up to the ground floor the estate agent guided us into the back room. The experience was tantamount to looking at an Imax screen, not that they existed back then. It wasn't a screen, though, it was one big window, and one with a truly wondrous view. In the foreground was the considerable expanse of the main pond on Hampstead Heath. Beyond that was the heath itself, with trees of all sizes and acres of green green grass. There were a few dogs and pram-pushers – presumably many of them mother's helps – but we were protected from them by the expanse of water. You couldn't see another house, although presumably our neighbours enjoyed a similar view. What's more, there were birds on and around the pond. Mallards, Tufted Ducks, a Coot on its nest and a pair of Great Crested Grebes displaying, framed by the overhanging fronds of a large willow. It had the kind of tree which my birding experience so far had taught me was bound to appeal to little birds, such as tit flocks and warblers. In future years indeed it did, along with Pied Flycatchers, Wood Warblers and Common Redstarts. Jean and I gazed out of that back window with the sunlight twinkling on the water. It felt as if we were on a boat. We were sold. So was the house.

The accountant who advised me to buy that house is sadly long gone but I will forever thank him since, as well as the good years, its ever-soaring value saw me through divorce without either Jean or I having to sell up, move out and start again. Indeed, I was able to afford the smaller house next door for Jean (not the concrete one) and a terraced house not overlooking but still pretty near to the heath for me and… I'll come to that shortly.

For a few years in the 1970s, whenever I was asked if we had a garden, I would rather smugly and yet truthfully reply: 'Yes. Hampstead Heath.'

'Yes but apart from that, have you got your own garden?'

'Well yes, but there's not much to it, but then we don't really need it.'

'No, but what's it like?'

South Hill Park

The garden was no wider than the house itself. It was basically on two levels and completely concreted over – maybe there had been a few bags left over from the neighbours' modernisation. There were railings across the end and it was an irresistible temptation to lean on them and stare across the water as if on the *Titanic*. In fact I do recall one moonlit canoodle that developed into something a little more raunchy, which led inexorably to the soft turf of the orchard that was accessible only by negotiating a small iron ladder down to the edge of the pond and tiptoeing together along the shore to the garden of delights. Actually it was all a bit clumsy and we had to watch out for nettles, but it was fun. Incidentally, the lady was not my wife, who by then had a boyfriend and spent a lot of time away doing what was then called agitprop theatre (activist, feminist, or politically correct). I was also away quite a bit filming *The Goodies* and appearing on *Top of the Pops* (not so politically correct).

In case you are about to accuse us of neglecting our daughters, we still had a mother's help, and when Jean moved next door the main house became sort of a commune. None of Miles Davis's band lived there, but we did have several jazz musicians, plus writers, actors, teachers and, as far as I recall, absolutely no layabouts or druggies. You see, oh non-believers, the 1970s were actually pretty cool.

Yes, but what about the garden? Well, like I said, there were two small concrete terraces. There may have been a few plant pots, which were nurtured by Jean, and I have a vague memory of growing tomatoes on bamboo sticks. Well Jean did. My roles tended to be to make things or to pay for things. We may have been the only house in London (or indeed anywhere) to have a cat-flap eight feet up on a wall. There were a couple of reasons for this. Firstly, you have to accept that you can't put a cat-flap in a glass French window. Secondly, it doesn't solve anything if a dozy builder puts it in the wall of a cloakroom that is on the second floor. Which is where I took over, and constructed a cat-ramp from the cloakroom flap down to the garden, and back up if the cat wanted to get back inside. The arrangement was particularly entertaining for anyone sitting outside on the terrace, who could enjoy the cat's wobbly ascent, or better still watch it come sliding down the ramp, or best of all when anyone suddenly felt a cat on their head and wondered where it had come from. By the way, I would like to stress that any house cats were not mine, they were Jean's. If you were hoping for a birder's vehement cat attack, fear not, there will be one later!

My other fatherly function was of course to purchase things the children couldn't possible live without. Nowadays, it would be a mobile phone. In the 1970s it was a trampoline. Comparing those two, I will bet on the trampoline lasting longest before it gets lost, broken, or dropped down the loo. Trampolines must be truly child-proof. I bought a big one. So big that it completely filled the concrete terrace. All four sides were touching something. One was up against next door's fence. Another had a narrow path against it which led down to the ladder that led to the orchard of love. The third side was on a level with the top terrace, and the fourth side – picture this if you will – was right up against the iron railings, which were of course originally introduced as a safety measure to prevent little kids, or tipsy adults, or even cats, from falling over onto the edge of the pond. The shoreline was by no means a soft landing since it was strewn not only with frogs and ducklings, but also with discarded tins and bottles and even the occasional randy couple. The railings worked. No one took a tumble. No one attempted to climb or jump. But what if you took off from a great big bouncy trampoline?

Surely we must have had house meetings about it. Where were health and safety when you needed them? Nowadays they're everywhere, in the Seventies nowhere. I shall never forget the scene I encountered when I arrived home to find a kids' party in full swing. The only sour note was that a little girl had scratched her knee. Otherwise, all was merriment and perpetual motion. There were at least a dozen boys and girls bouncing and leaping and inevitably competing with each other to see who could get the highest. Adult parties often had much the same goal.

They began to dare each other. 'I bet I can bounce over the railings, down onto the shoreline.'

Countered by 'I bet I can bounce over the railings, right into the pond.'

Capped by 'Straight into the jaws of a Pike!'

And believe me there were some big 'uns in there. As it happens, the divine custodian of hyperactive kids literally dampened their spirits by releasing a summer thunderstorm and everyone ran inside screaming and panicking. But honestly, kids on a trampoline could crash onto concrete. Or soar over the railings and plummet into the water. Pike or no Pike, I can barely believe we let it happen. Or was that what we did in the Seventies? Whatever the case we got away with it. Nobody died.

There was a short period towards the end of the 1970s when the goings on at that house sounded like something from a sitcom. I believe somebody did write a TV series called *My Wife Next Door*. I don't remember seeing it, but it can't have been as bizarre as our set up. Jean literally did live next door, except that there was an adjoining door between the two houses. The kids could come and go as they pleased. So could Jean. She frequently appeared on my side of the wall without notice or warning. To be honest I didn't really mind, but what I did mind was that the arrangement was not reciprocal. If I wanted to cross over to the other side I had to give several hours notice or send a written application. This didn't bother me much either, since the purpose of going next door was often to have a row. The arguments sometimes ended with something being thrown at me – on one occasion half a house brick. I think that was a sure sign that our attempts to stay together for the children should finally be abandoned. This decision was duly discussed by the members of the commune, who graciously accepted that they would soon be house-hunting themselves. Some have stayed friends, others haven't.

I have mentioned nothing about the garden by the heath. There wasn't much to it. You can't put plant pots on a trampoline. I don't recall Jean ever mentioning gardening. It was only many many years later that I realised that she must have felt somewhat deprived. Much to our mutual satisfaction, and maybe with a touch of pride, after new lives with new partners and new houses, we are regularly in touch and there is no acrimony whatsoever about the past. Jean has a house only a mile or two from mine and – this is the point – she has designed, planted and maintains an exquisite garden. It is small and square with no room for a lawn or flowerbeds, and yet it is a riot of colour and imagination. She is expert at acquiring small trees and shrubs, which unfailingly thrive and blossom. Silky clematis climb the walls, which are of course painted white in true Mediterranean style, and there are exotic blooms, that – coincidentally I am sure – often appear after she has had a day at Kew Gardens. She even knows most of the Latin names, which I have to demand that she anglicises when we are having a discussion… Yes, gardening. Isn't that one of life's little ironies?

It has taken 50 years to discover we share the same enthusiasm.

Just about to discover
a Dunnock's nest?

Above: Bill and mum
Below: Me and my dad. I am already wearing a Fair Isle cardigan, presumably thinking 'one day I shall go to Fair Isle and find a Pallas's Reed Bunting.

Above: Dad looking smart.

Below: Dad at Poole Harbour in Dorset. Was he birdwatching?

Above: The author (bottom right) aged about 9.

Below: Ringing Puffins on the Farne Islands, Northumberland.

My current garden in all its glory.
The shed has a green roof courtesy
of Enterprise Plants.

It is always the same with tins and jars. Can't get 'em open.

To me it's a moth trap, to the Robins it's a fast-food cafe.

Robin, Dunnock and miniature croc. Living together in perfect harmony.

I don't suppose you can do anything
about Cyprus and Malta?

Robin exploring my living room, posing with toucan and monarchs.

Juvenile Robin perusing the moth menu. "I'd try a Lesser Broad-bordered Yellow Underwing. Or maybe a Snout."

Robin. Do you realise one of us must be a reflection?

Robin caught in the shed stealing mealworms.

Britain's National Bird?
Not looking like this!

This picture shows a gorilla and a
Robin. Can you tell which is which?

'Is that meant to be a cat?'

My garden nemesis.
The phantom feline.

Original artwork depicting the Loch Ness Monster swallowing a hedgehog. Note the genuine woodpecker hole, which used to be much higher.

Makes a change from Robins.

All that headbutting their own reflection can't do Dunnocks any good.

A Blackbird's impression of a Puffin.

Above: Parakeets on red berries. But they still don't look Christmassy.

Below: Parakeet and broken glass ornament

Above: Parakeets against a tinted Hampstead sky.

Below: Who really is 'the King' as far as the birds are concerned?

Mummy told me to stay in the shed so people won't laugh at me!

What is he eating?
Bill Oddie's fat balls of course.

Try Again

Couples gardening together sounds delightfully idyllic, but I wonder whether it is natural, or maybe even possible. I suspect that Jean was always green-fingered, but she wouldn't want me interfering. Nor indeed would I have wanted to interfere. Once I was out of the way she was free to burgeon.

Supporting the same theory, my second wife Laura showed little interest in our new garden. Perhaps because I wouldn't let her? Maybe because I wanted to stamp my own style on it? After all, for the first time in my life I referred to it as my garden.

Our new house didn't overlook Hampstead Heath, but it was only five minutes' walk away. When we moved in the back garden, which is about the size of half a tennis court, was frankly a bit of a mess. There was little or no evidence of husbandry. The small square lawn had obviously been strimmed rather than mowed and a raised flowerbed was flowerless.

There was a creaky old shed at the end, and opposite it the most puzzling feature, a concrete patio which wasn't even big or safe enough for a small trampoline. A clue to its intended function was a couple of collapsed deckchairs, so presumably it was a place for lounging in the sun. Except that there wasn't any sun. Not just that day. Not ever. It was facing the wrong way. Nevertheless, I saw the opportunity and the challenge to create a garden feature I had always wanted – a pond.

Get A Man In

When faced with a new garden with clay soil full of rubble and with an unsightly and sunless concrete platform in one corner, it is possible that many people would resort to a little practical advice and possibly even some professional help to at least get the transformation started. In our house this is referred to as 'getting a man in' and – except in exceptionally specialist dangerous circumstances – I refuse to condone it. I appreciate that Laura has two motives for arguing otherwise, one being that the man may do a good job, and two that I won't electrocute myself, or fall off a ladder, or out of a window I am leaning out of to get at a mains pipe. For most of our thirty years of marriage I have avoided serious injuries and Laura has, I think, accepted that there are some sections of ceiling that will never ever get painted. On my part, I like to think that I have become slightly more accepting that 'getting a man in' is sensible on a few special occasions. For example, installing a new central heating boiler, or replacing a large section of collapsed ceiling, or indeed trying to track down the source of damp in the back wall of the bedroom. All are tasks that I reluctantly accept are probably beyond me. Mind you, tracing the origins of the damp has also been beyond all the men we have got in so far. Nevertheless, I am confident that some day it will be found. What's more, it will be I who find it. Furthermore, I may well be able to fix it too. After all 'I am a man. M. A. N.'

Get A Man Out

The main 'get a man in' discussion/argument occurs with some regularity, but only to do with issues related to the house or the equipment therein. Laura knows better than to ever suggest that a man is got in for anything to do with the garden. This principle was established long long ago on the day I announced that I was going to make a garden pond.

Laura was understandably alarmed. 'Are you going to dig up the lawn?'

'No, I am going to destroy that patio.'

'Isn't it solid concrete?'

'Yes,' I replied.

'Wouldn't it be best to… ?'

'Don't even think it. When it comes to my garden I will never ever get a man in.'

'Not even a man with a pneumatic drill?'

'Nope. I shall do it myself with an old sledge hammer I have found in the shed.' And I did. Over a couple of days I swung my hammer like a blues singer working on the railroad, until I had dug a hole roughly six-feet square. I didn't even get a man in with a skip. I shoveled the spoil into corners of the garden to create more variable heights, and the less unsightly chunks of concrete became the basis of rockeries. That started a habit that I still continue. I have never bought 'ornamental' rocks from garden centres. Instead, I lurk around building sites and roadworks and pop portable pieces into my pocket or my brief case. I have a small rockery built entirely from the rubble left by British Rail when the banks of a nearby cutting caved in. Some of our neighbours down the road literally lost their gardens overnight, but mine got bigger.

The next task was waterproofing my potential pond. Our road is built on deep London Clay and for a few seconds I did consider puddling it in the pond, but that would require more digging, and frankly my back was beginning to protest. Besides which, I didn't know what puddling was but I assumed it would entail a lot of crouching and bending. I was not so stubborn that I even shunned shopping at a garden centre, so I drove down to our local and purchased a large roll of butyl liner. The excitement was mounting. I hadn't built a pond before and I didn't have an instruction leaflet, but I was sure I knew what to do. There are not that many choices. First dig the hole – done. Then cover the soil – especially if there are jaggedy stones in it – using newspaper, old carpet or moth-eaten rugs, of which there are always plenty around when you move house. Then spread the sheet of butyl across the hole, hoping that it's the right size. Gently push and adjust it, so that it clings to the contours, then smooth out the edges around the lip of the hole, again hoping that it's big enough. Weigh down the edges of the liner with heavy stones. Now take a very deep breath and listen to your heart thumping. It is filling time. Only gardeners and reservoir workers know this thrill. In goes the hose, out comes the water. It takes forever. Finally, it is nearly full. Now here comes a moment of huge satisfaction or horrible frustration. The water has risen to the lip on one side of the pond, but is at least six inches lower than the other side. It isn't level. Probably you should have used a spirit level, but it is not a total disaster. There are a few things you can do. You can cry. Or you can laugh hollowly. You can accept that one bank will always be lower or higher than the other, and you can resolve to disguise the banks with more rocks and aquatic plants so that it won't be immediately obvious.

This is fine, as long as you accept that you will never ever totally cover the edges of the butyl lining. Or – here's the brave option – you can heave up a corner of the lining, pour away the water – you won't believe how much there is – and wade around in your wellies carefully digging out more clay and constantly judging the levels. Whilst doing this try not to puncture the butyl, because if you do it is 'start again' time. The results of my labours on my very first pond were pretty satisfying. The shoreline was only slightly uneven, and I buried the visible butyl banks with piles of soil. The whole thing looked almost natural, if a little sparse, and of course it didn't get the sun.

That pond is still there. I confess that it eventually it sprang a leak which I couldn't mend, because I couldn't find it. It was a muddy old palaver but I tugged out the butyl and replaced it with a large moulded plastic pond which I laid into the hole of the original one. The current version is a hybrid. It has a plastic pond in the middle with a little fountain. This nestles in the slightly larger space of the original pond, which is hardly an inch deep but supports a splendid little reedbed, Purple Loosestrife, and a stately stand of Yellow Irises. This mini-marsh is the habitat of a lone Glossy Ibis, which is not only glossy but also fake. More of such things later.

MY Garden

From that day to this my garden has been a hobby, a distraction, a challenge, an outlet for my own peculiar brand of creativity, a godsend, a therapy and a delight. If I have been away from home, the first thing I do is scamper out into the garden and start frantically sniffing around rather like Delilah, my daughter's hyperactive Jack Russell. Mind you, Delilah doesn't feed the birds, which is the second thing I do.

Laura and I are still here in the same house. I was going to say in the same garden, but inevitably it has changed quite a lot. When our daughter Rosie was a toddler it was of course a play place, often with little friends who occasionally had sleepovers in a tent on the lawn. They usually lasted about an hour before someone got scared or needed a wee. In Rosie's early teenage years there were teenage parties. I will say no more about them for fear of reviving traumatic memories for us and probably for some of you. They eventually abated but we then spent so many angst-ridden hours wondering where the kids were that we almost wished we could go back to the days – and nights – with vodka bottles in the flowerbeds and fag ends in the pond. However, I could sense that the time was nigh when I would be able to reclaim my territory. I had every intention of making it reflect my own personality as I saw it: lively but bloody stupid, yet creative with it. That is what I have been doing ever since.

Blame It On Orlando

It all started with a mouse. Walt Disney was extremely fond of those words. The mouse in question was of course Mickey and the 'it' was the whole of the Disney Empire from *Steamboat Willie* to the Disney World Leisure Resorts. What Walt never realised was that much the same thing applied to my garden, which in turn reflects the style of our house. In fact it was undoubtedly Laura's fault, although I willingly share the credit, or the blame.

It all began in Florida many years ago. Laura and I were a relatively new couple, not yet married and perhaps at that stage when you are enthusing about one another's suggestions and tastes, whilst not actually admitting that you totally disagree with them. The confessional may not emerge for many many years, usually with the words 'You know, I never did like that...' whatever it is. Most revelations don't matter too much, but start worrying if one of the things that your partner 'never liked' includes you! I am happy to say that after 30 years of marriage we still haven't got to that stage. Well, not often.

Meanwhile, back in the days when we were young lovers choosing the destination for our very first holiday together, Florida seemed a pretty safe bet. Laura had to put up with me reminiscing about what a great week I had had there with Jean after our stage tour of America in 1964. Laura, however, was not one to let a few twinges of jealousy spoil the recommendation of a perfect holiday spot. Jean and I may have had a good time, but Laura and I would have a better one. Inevitably, I raved about the profusion of birds and other wildlife. In itself I doubt that it was of any consequence to her, but at least she seemed pleased that my birding obsession would be satisfied. I diluted my slight feeling of selfish guilt by reassuring us both that many of the best bird places were also scenically delightful. I regaled her with tales of silver-sanded beaches and undeveloped shorelines, as well as miles of lakes, swamps and waterways, which one could explore by canoe or hydrofoil. I didn't even bother to make an accommodation reservation. No need, I assured Laura. 'We'll fly to Miami, get a hire car and then drive across to the Gulf Coast. It's a lovely drive – a coast road, parallel to the sea, and every now and then there will be a cosy little motel literally on the beach. It's unspoilt and uncrowded.' Well, it was in 1964. Alas, by the time Laura and I got there the motels had melded together and most of them had grown into hotels – several of them multistorey – or worse still, soulless blocks of rental apartments which Americans call 'condos,' which is at least a marginally more giggle-worthy word than 'condominium,' which sounds like a health spa in Ancient Rome. As we drove south we caught occasional glimpses of blue water, although not much of it was open sea since the other thing that hadn't been there in 1964 was mile after mile of marinas.

It wasn't a jolly drive, especially for Laura since she had to put up with my constant audible disgruntlement and disappointment as I recalled delights that were no longer there or had changed beyond recognition. 'There's a lovely jetty round this corner. Well, there was. Not any more.' 'There used to be lots of tidal bays, really good for waders. Now it's a marina.' To add to my grumpiness every motel we passed had a 'no vacancies' sign on it. On and on we drove. Me muttering my discontent and Laura presumably thinking 'Do I really want to be with such a whinger.' We eventually found accommodation in a fifth-floor room with no sea view, in what purported to be a Holiday Inn. That's what it said on the sign. However, it may have been *a* holiday inn, but it certainly wasn't *the* Holiday Inn I had envisaged. Whatever it was it bore little resemblance to the bijou little beach motel where Jean and I had stayed in '64. Sorry Laura.

We spent the next two days driving round the interior of central Florida with me failing to find various wetlands and reedbeds that I had visited on my previous trip. Some of them were even still mentioned in *A Birders' Guide to Florida*. Some of them I found, but they were now built up or had been transformed into commercial waterways. Others had disappeared. The biggest blow of all was that I couldn't find Lake Okeechobee. Lake Okeechobee gets lots of pages in any Florida guidebook. It is huge — it always has been, no doubt was then, and I hope it still is. There is room for both watersports and waterbirds, and I daresay that there are trail leaflets and information boards. What state it was in when I drove around looking for it with Laura I don't know, because I couldn't find it. For an entire morning I tied our hire car in knots, doing three-point turns, getting stuck in cul-de-sacs, and becoming hotter and crosser. Both of us. The debacle culminated when I pulled off onto yet another lay-by from which I could just about catch a distant glimpse of a sliver of lake and the flag on the mast of a yacht that was otherwise totally invisible, gliding slowly beyond a screen of tall dense reeds. 'It's a bit like the Norfolk Broads,' I muttered. 'There are places you can't get at there too.'

Meanwhile, Laura leant on the car and stared into the far beyond. She was clearly not enjoying herself. Her look said 'I am not happy.' Her voice asked 'Are we going to do this for the rest of the week?' I apologised and I certainly didn't say 'Yes' or even 'Maybe.' Instead I asked her, as I should've done days ago, 'Is there something you would rather do?'

She replied with a question that in truth I was slightly dreading: 'How far are we from Disney World?'

'Er, not that far. Why?'

'Because I have always wanted to go to Disney World. You know that.'

It was now my turn to flinch. It was true, I did sort of know that she wanted to go to Disney World. But I definitely didn't. However, rather than qualify for the prize of the World's Wettest Blanket, I reacted with a cautious response that might well have turned out to be true. 'I don't know if we can get accommodation in Disney World.' That much was true. I didn't know. Until I tried. After a couple of hours on the phone I was able to triumphantly announce that we had a double room for three nights *inside* Walt Disney World Resort. No morning car queues. No shuttle buses. We would be right there.

Laura perused the brochure. 'Is it a Tree House Villa?'

'No.'

'Or the Grand Floridian?'

'No. Everything was full, but I've got us into the golf hotel!'

I daresay Laura wasn't ecstatic, but at least I didn't play golf. In fact it turned out to be rather nice. Only a couple of storeys high and, surprise surprise, surrounded by golf courses with sandy bunkers, greens and roughs, lots of small lakes, and a fair selection of the sorts of birds that I had failed to find at Okeechobee.

Laura declared it infinitely preferable to staying in a seedy motel or sweltering in the car. She was particularly delighted to discover that the transport around Disney World was impeccably efficient, and free. There were buses and monorails, and in fact the 'golf hotel' was within walking distance of the Travel Centre, which was the gateway to The Magic Kingdom and beyond. Laura loved it and, guess what, so did I. I enjoyed the best of both Disney World and the natural world as it was immediately evident that birds aren't the remotest bit fazed or spooked by speedboats, Mississippi steamboats, or even human-sized Mickeys, Goofys and Donalds zooming around on water-skis. I will admit that actors in animal suits freak me out, but the birds don't seem to care. I am sure that anyone who has been to Florida's Disney World will confirm that there is plenty of good birding to be enjoyed without ever having to leave the park. On subsequent visits – and there were several – I discovered that an early morning stroll along a canal was likely to produce a mixed warbler and vireo flock, and that in the evening the car park turned into a huge roosting site for Yellow-rumped Warblers – the warbler formerly known as Myrtle. There were invariably vultures circling around the tower of Snow White's Castle, and one early autumn sprinklers on the golfing greens turned them into perfect if temporary wader habitat, where I got some decent photos of dowitchers, yellowlegs and sandpipers, as well as a telling off by a ranger. Very politely. Disney doesn't do anger. 'It's for your own safety sir. Some of our senior clients are, let's say, not entirely accurate.' I agreed. A lot of them could barely stand upright. Added to which they certainly shouldn't be in sole charge of a golf buggy. After being run down three times in one morning I decided to stay off the greens. I was rewarded with my best Disney bird, an incomparably graceful Swallow-tailed Kite.

Inspired by Mickey

What, I sense you wondering, has all this got to do with my new garden in North London? Okay, the thing is that Disney World is divided up into areas, or 'lands,' with appropriate names such as Fantasyland, Adventureland, Frontierland, and so on. Within these areas are such features as Pleasure Island (not that sort of pleasure of course), Discovery Island (a sort of walk-through menagerie), and more. At some point during or shortly after a Disney holiday, Laura and I mutually decided to redecorate and furnish our house by creating themed rooms and areas. The kitchen encapsulated the concept by having a whole wall full of shelves with Disney merchandise and memorabilia, including Mickeys and Minnies of all sizes. There were Mickey-faced teapots and telephones, crockery with a clever design incorporating Mickey's black stylised round ears, and — my favourite display — a shelf of shame, a rogue's gallery of what we christened 'Mickey Rats.' These misshapen creatures are the sorts of toys you find at the shops in departure lounges at distant airports, which have not been licensed by Disney and bear little resemblance to the official Mickey. Some of them bear very little resemblance to anything living. As an overall homage the only colours allowed in the kitchen were Mickey's – so red, yellow, black and white.

On the walls of the top landing Laura painted a mural of a deckchair on a beach at an English resort, thus transforming it into 'Seasideland.' The adjacent room was designated our 'Jungle Bedroom,' with green tropical foliage wallpaper that took us weeks to find – there was no Google or Amazon in those days. It is still hanging today. There are plastic daisies around the bamboo bedstead, and a selection of animals ranging from an almost life-sized fluffy tiger to a tiny pair of porcelain lovebirds.

At my own initiative I created what was meant to be a vineyard-themed bathroom. This involved tacking wooden trelliswork on the walls and festooning it with artificial flowers and leaves and lots of bunches of rubber grapes. I have to confess that it wasn't quite up to the standard of the other themes in the house and I suspect that Laura was rather embarrassed by it. It was not until 2016 that I finally gave the bathroom a total makeover. There are still a few grapes dangling off the shower but the trellis has been replaced by a sunny yellow paint which I have decorated with metal butterflies and lizards, while the shower door is now covered in those raptor silhouettes that are meant to stop birds from crashing into windows. I should be so lucky.

At some point in time through the years I think Laura and I must have come to a tacit agreement that any more Disney-influenced theme areas in the house should be left to her, because – let's face it – she is a far better artist than me. I have a modicum of technique, but very little of what most people would call taste. Logically therefore I am banned from experimenting inside the house. If I want to indulge my wacky ways I have to go outside into the garden, where I can do what I like.

What I Like

Nearly everything I do in my garden is guided by the themed areas principle. The first one to be created and christened was the pond. As quickly as I could coax them to grow, I had planted flag irises and marsh marigolds. I also positioned a couple of already reasonably sized palm-type trees, whose fronds cast even more shade over an already dappled corner. I also planted a spindly anorexic willow which over the years has exceeded all expectations and is currently threatening to reach the top-floor windows of our neighbours' houses and obliterate sunlight from the entire street.

Undoubtedly this corner resembled a small section of rainforest. I named it Vietnam and fixed a wooden sign close by. Some years later, to commemorate a wonderful trip to see Orang-utans in the wild, I renamed it Borneo.

At least my mini-Borneo doesn't look completely incongruous in a book about gardens in that it is largely green and growing. This cannot be said for the corner I call 'Inca Ruins.' I think it was inspired by acquiring one of those terracotta suns with a face and spikey flame-like hair. Frankly I don't know whether they really are based on Inca ritual sculpture, or if they are just a cliché bestseller at garden centres. In any event, I associated anything terracotta with the Incas, and had a ready supply of building materials in the form of pieces of broken plant pots, a shattered vase which actually came from Crete, and a pile of discarded old house bricks which I arranged to resemble a small section of collapsed wall, which was all that remained of an ancient building possibly damaged by an earthquake (not a Hampstead earthquake, of course). No plants grow amongst the rubble. It wasn't a huge leap of imagination to decide on a concept of an ancient ruin and it has remained undisturbed for many years, except for the addition of a couple of well-weathered Easter Island statues, and a notice of more recent vintage proclaiming that this area is also known as 'The Rat Run.' This refers to a story told in full later on in the book.

Closer to the house and indeed intentionally visible through our large back windows is the Magic Tree. It is actually a lilac which, like all lilacs, looks fabulous for about two days a year and then rapidly goes rusty and is frankly quite unsightly. I resolved to brighten it up a bit. My inspiration was my first trip to India in the early 1980s. It is a cliché, and therefore true, to say that India is a land of extreme contrasts. Abject poverty and sumptuous wealth, overwhelming overpopulation and inspirational solitude. Some sights that are shockingly gross and others that are breathtakingly beautiful. As we – four birdwatchers – drove south out of Delhi on our first morning, it became rapidly and entertainingly clear that Indian people are very fond of colour, decoration and sparkle. Most roadside trees were no doubt so bombarded with petrol fumes that they struggled to bear leaves, let alone blossom, but no matter, the nearest street vendor or owner of a roadside ramshackle shack, had festooned the naked branches with just about anything that could hang, flutter, twinkle, tinkle or glow. The *Blue Peter* team would have been impressed by the imaginative and creative recycling of ribbons, string, tins, bottles, silver paper, fag packets and so on. I dubbed them 'Magic Trees,' the magic being the ingenuity and joy illuminating such a potentially grim setting. It is this concept that I have attempted to transfer to my lilac in Hampstead, not that I am implying that Hampstead is in any way grim.

Not every item on my Magic Tree is recycled, but many of them are broken. I am always loathe to throw anything away, especially if it will reflect light. Talking of light, the centrepiece is a quite large ballroom glitterball, which when it reflects the rays of the morning sun sends cascades of sunbeams whirling round the garden and even onto the ceiling of our back room. At first it can be quite confusing. It feels as if you are being attacked by fireflies. Or at least momentarily transported to the main ballroom at Blackpool Tower, which is the only ballroom that I have ever been in, when dad took me there as a teenager. Why? I have no idea. I suppose he may have been reliving some romantic moment from his youth.

I would never claim that the Magic Tree is remotely romantic. One branch is decorated entirely in defunct kitchen utensils, especially the silvery ones like cheese graters, soup spoons and a small colander. There are some of those twisty dangly plastic things you get in New Age shops and a few mini-wind chimes. Some would call it all very hippie-ish.

I wouldn't deny it. In fact I am rather proud of it. India in the Seventies. I was there.

If the Magic Tree is defiantly light-hearted, the area by the door on the other side of the garden is downright peculiar. Its theme is gloom and doom. It is known as Spooky Corner and it resembles a section of the set from the film *Carrie* or maybe TV's *True Blood*. Laura once equated my creation of Spooky Corner with my first symptoms of clinical depression. I disputed this, if only on the grounds that when I was in a depression I could do absolutely nothing except lay in bed and weep or sleep. The last thing I was capable of was working in the garden constructing a complex tableau. Mind you, albeit that I protested that it was just a bit of whimsy, I can well see how the ingredients may have appeared not so much whimsical as weird. There is a small chunk of iron fencing like you get in graveyards. I think I got it off a skip. Well, I hope so. It has a plastic owl perched on top and a rubber snake wound round it. The centrepiece is a pair of juju sticks with skulls on top. I think my daughter bought or stole them from a rock festival. Perhaps the most disturbing feature is a white porcelain hand which I made look as if it is reaching up from under the earth (remember *Carrie?*). Even I was a little shocked that I deemed it necessary to apply a dribble of red paint to look like blood running down the fingers. As well as the main features Spooky Corner was, and still is, populated by a number of spiders, bats and snakes. None of them real of course. Oh yes, appropriately, I am sure you will agree, I have sprayed the whole display frosty white. This includes a reclining gnome who is sort of the keeper of the corner. Instead of a guard dog by his side, he has a white mole.

The Little People

Talking of gnomes... The most traditional theme-park inspired feature of the garden, and I think the most impressive one to most visitors, is Gnome Corner. I have long subscribed to the principle that whilst a single gnome is fine, two are better, ten much better, and thirty or forty are when it starts to get fun. My Gnome Corner has just over a hundred. Of course it started with one, but increased more rapidly than you might imagine. It all began at our wedding party, which was held where else but in the garden.

We had sent out a very specific instruction to our family and friends. 'Please do not bring us traditional wedding presents. For example, we do not need canteens of cutlery, antique cruets, or embroidered napkins. Let's face it, we have been living together for a few years so we have probably bought whatever we want or need for ourselves. We also wish to save you the trauma of trying to think of something really unusual, which we might not like anyway. Therefore dear guest we are simply asking you, or telling you: Please bring us a gnome.'

Quite a few people simply couldn't do it. We got phone calls asking: 'Do you mean a garden gnome?'

To which surely the only response is: 'Do you know of any non-garden gnomes?'

Other people simply chose to ignore our request. I can imagine that scenario: 'They are getting a canteen of cutlery, and that's it.'

'Oh darling that's just because that's what they gave us.'

'Have we ever used it?'

'No.'

'Or the napkins?'

'No, but we can't give them those – they'll recognise them.'

'What, from five years ago?'

'Darling.'

'What now?'

'Maybe it would be quite fun to take a gnome.'

Quite fun. I should say so. I am not sure whether we'd not told people that we'd asked everyone to bring a gnome, or whether they just couldn't believe it. The first couple arrived and duly proudly placed their gnome in the middle of a large circular space I had covered in gravel. Surely this was a clue that gnome number one would soon acquire a little friend. He duly did. And another and another. There were little ones and big ones, lightweight plastic ones and concrete ones that were almost too heavy to carry. Applause and laughter accompanied each new arrival. Little matching groups began to emerge, proving the point that whilst one gnome can be rather twee, a little team of identical gnomes gets funnier and funnier. Did you ever see that episode of *Till Death Us Do Part* when the house was totally invaded by gnomes?

The people I felt a bit sorry for were the ones who came tottering down the alley carrying a huge stone gnome. Surely there must be a point at which a gnome gets too big to be a gnome? The giver of a new arrival staggered in proudly boasting: 'I bet you haven't got one of these. Oh.' And their faces fell as they spied a gaggle of identical big stone gnomes. At least they received some sympathy from the others. New friends were made, and even the canteen of cutlery types were heard berating their partners for refusing to let them do the gnome thing. I fear we might have spoilt a few marriages, as well as giving ours a great start. What's more, it is a gift that has kept on giving.

By the end of the wedding party Gnome Corner housed nearly one hundred inhabitants. It is a community that has remained pretty much stable for the past three decades. Some really old fellas have passed on, shattered by a clumsy boot or a wayward spade. Many of them I have repainted, even sometimes changing their traditional colours and giving them yellow caps or purple pants. Like the Aztec ruins, Gnome Corner is of no horticultural interest. The plants that do invade the territory tend to be of the not really wild kind, like Green Alkanet and Nettle-leaved Bellflower. Both are worth allowing to blossom a bit before pulling them up. Every now and then I have to clear out these self-seeders before they obliterate the view. You would be surprised how easy it is to hide a hundred gnomes.

Gardening Areas

By now you have no doubt deduced that I know very little about proper gardening. The bits that I do know I have learnt from being out in the countryside and the wild, and in particular those times when I have been in the company of a real botanist. Some time back in the 1980s I had what I could refer to as a floral breakthrough. Almost all my life until then I had been a birdwatcher. Frankly, yet shamefully, I very rarely noticed, let alone really looked at or tried to identify, anything but birds. I knew others who were just as insular. These days, however, many birders are equally adept at sorting out butterflies, dragonflies, moths and in fact just about anything and everything, although I still find spider-watchers a bit thin on the ground. Indeed, I myself would now claim to be a passable all-rounder and I spend as much time squinting at damselflies and grasshoppers as I do at birds. Even if I don't know all their names, I do know which book to look them up in or of course which website to visit.

This is all very much to the good. I have always claimed that broadening out beyond just birds was one of the best moves I ever made. It was even more satisfying to apply the same principle on TV. As *Birding with Bill Oddie* evolved into *How to Watch Wildlife* the truth was that I myself was discovering creatures and experiences that were new and fresh to me and hopefully I could 'take the audience with me.' It is significant that most of my favourite items did not involve birds, I suppose because I had been watching them all my life and seen not everything, but quite a lot. However, I was yet to spot my first Otter, or plunge my hand in a Wood Ants' nest, or swim – or rather flounder – with Grey Seals. Even handling and being gnawed by small rodents was curiously enjoyable, albeit excruciatingly painful. The bite of a Water Shrew was most agonising, but the Orkney Vole drew the most blood.

However, let's face it, when it comes to British mammals there are not a huge number to get your head or hands around. Not so with wildflowers. There are literally thousands. What I needed was a guide. I don't mean a 'Field Guide to the Wildflowers of Britain and Europe,' I mean a real expert patient human mentor. Thus in the summer of 1989 I headed for Hauxley Nature Reserve in Northumberland. Hauxley is one of those places whose very existence is almost symbolic of constructive conservation. Once upon a time it was an industrial blot on the landscape, scarred by years of open-cast mining. It would hardly have been undisturbed or peaceful. It must have been messy and nasty, unattractive to both birds and birders. However, as the coal ran out, the Northumberland Wildlife Trust moved in. The diggers and bulldozers started shoveling sand and shingle, reshaping the terrain into pools, muddy creeks and islands.

Conservationists are fond of quoting a line from the movie *Field of Dreams*: 'Build it and they will come.' In the film it refers to building a baseball pitch to conjure the return of legendary pitchers and batters. In the conservation world it refers to creating a habitat to attract whatever you wish to entice. The beauty of it is that it works, both with the ghosts of baseball players and with nature.

In late June 1989 I set off to Northumberland and drove north from Newcastle, parallel to the classic coastline of Druridge Bay, which incidentally – even as I type – is being threatened by, would you believe, open-cast mining. Please God, by the time you are reading this the area will have been declared an untouchable reserve once and for all. In 1989 it was the early days of regenerating the area and changing the priority from extracting coal to attracting wildlife. As I recall, the main Druridge Bay area in those days was simply and rather gloriously 'empty,' even bleak when the wind was coming off the North Sea. However, Hauxley is a delightful little reserve with lots to look at. As ever, my main quest was to search for birds, but as I entered the car park my eye was caught by a large grassy bank glowing with masses of purple orchids (even I knew that much). As I walked to the visitor centre, which was little more than a humble hut, I passed a small circular wildflower meadow. A 'raised bed,' I think gardeners would call it. Butterflies and bees zoomed around the flowering plants, which I assumed correctly were a small selection of what was growing on the main reserve. Some I had seen before, perhaps growing in a hedgerow, or more likely providing a perch for a bird, but most I didn't recognise. I needed my guide. At that moment, Nick the Hauxley warden appeared. He offered me tea but I politely refused, as

I always do since I can never resist the urge to get out immediately to see 'what's about.' Tea, coffee and sandwiches can all wait. Of course this impatience is relevant to birds, but not to flowers, which do not fly away. I suspect that Nick was amused, maybe even impressed by my almost childish enthusiasm. In fact I suspect that he had anticipated it, since he had already packed a pocket with the traditional naturalist's snack of a bottle of water and a Mars bar.

As we walked down the path to the main lake I asked if there were any good birds around. His response surprised and intrigued me.

'I'll be honest, Bill. I am not much of a birder. Botany is my thing.'

At that moment the bargain was struck. We had a day to enlighten each other. I would teach him the birds and he would teach me the flowers.

You Show Me Yours

As we wandered around Hauxley it became clear that the tasks weren't entirely even. The bird identification didn't go much further than sorting out Redshank, Greenshank and Ruff, while Nick admitted that he already knew Lapwing, Oystercatcher, Shelduck and Coot. That was my job done.

A few hundred flowers might be a bit more of a challenge. Nick was a very good teacher. He showed me some of the flower families, usually letting me lead by pointing at something and inviting me to take a guess.

'Er, I'd call that a vetch,' I replied.

'Good. It is. And that one?'

'Another kind of vetch?'

'Yes,' confirmed Nick.

'Which kind?'

'I'll tell you later.'

'What about the yellow one?' I asked.

'Not quite the same, but in the same family. Well done. They are all called legumes.'

Suddenly I was back doing French oral. 'Legumes? Vegetables, right? So what kind of vegetables?'

'They've got little pods.'

'Like peas? And beans?'

'Exactly. So we'll look out for legumes.'

'Mais oui, fantastique. And can we have a look at the orchids? Ahh. Oui oui, formidable. Elles sont tres jolies.'

I was soon on my hands and knees crouched amongst the purple spikes trying to spot any differences. They all looked much the same.

'Do you want to have a guess?' challenged Nick.

'Er, Purple Orchid?'

'Nearly, that's Early Purple Orchid.'

'But it's the end of June. That's not early.'

'Ah, it is up north. They'd be much earlier down in Devon, say.'

'So these are all Early Purples?'

'No, there's also Northern Marsh Orchid. That's this one. And Common Spotted Orchid. They look very similar.'

'They look exactly the same!'

'In fact,' Nick explained, 'quite a few of these are hybrids.'

'Hybrids?'

Nick sensed my impending panic. 'Ah now that's a different one. It's shaped like a what?'

'A pyramid.'

'And it is called a Pyramidal Orchid.'

'Good name. And it doesn't hybridise?'

'No.'

'Even better. You know, Nick, I much prefer these orchids to the ones you get at weddings and funerals.'

'They are not remotely related. Sure you don't fancy a cuppa tea?'

You bet I did. We retired to the reception hut. As I sipped I leafed through a British flower book enjoying the variety of shapes and colours, but wincing at the sections which seemed to have several pages of flowers that looked almost identical. For example, there were yellow ones that all looked more or less like dandelions, but had totally different names. Nick pointed at them in the book and admitted that those can be a bit tricky.

'Those are mainly hawkweeds.'

'Hawkweed. Why's it called that?' I asked.

'People used to think it helped their eyesight.'

'Why?'

'Because hawks have incredible eyesight,' said Nick.

'Yes they do. And do hawks feed on these flowers?'

'No they don't.'

'Don't they?'

'No, but maybe someone saw one once and made the connection. And you know how folklore spreads.'

'No I don't actually.' I have never understood how folklore spreads. I mean, come on, this was way before newspapers – no post, no phones, no social media. And yet some bloke somewhere sees a Kestrel drop down into the grass – probably after a vole actually – but he thinks it's eating the yellow flowers. So the bloke thinks maybe that's good for its eyes. Down the tavern that evening he's had a few pints of ale and he starts going on about hawks.

'Incredible eyesight, hawks.'

'Oh incredible,' all his mates agree.

'My theory is it's what they eat that's good for their eyes.'

'What, voles? Eating voles is good for your eyes?'

'No no. I have been watching a Kestrel in my field and I can tell you he or she – dunno which – consumes large quantities of yellow flowers.'

'Dandelions?'

'Ah no. They are not dandelions, I dunno what they are. They probably haven't got a name. In which case, I shall commemorate their remarkable properties of improving our eyesight.'

'Our eyesight?'

'Yeah, you know that expression he's got eyes like a hawk? If you keep eating those yellow flowers you will have. I thereby name them hawkweeds.'

'You know something Jethro, that could become folklore.'

And before you know it, they're passing it round the pubs. It's all round London, Scotland, Wales, Ireland. Until some charlatan of an 18th century medicine man who goes round the country gathering crackpot remedies publishes it in his latest apothecary and flogs bottles of the stuff.

'Ladies and gents, are you myopic or just fuzzy round the edges? Don't you wish you had eyes like a Kestrel?'

'What, bright yellow?'

'No, to get incredible eyesight, drink elixir of hawkweed.

Hawkweed, also available as an infusion, or you can just bite the flower off and chew it. Roll up. Roll up. Cheaper than Specsavers.'

Now, lest I be accused of facetiousness, I am of course not disputing that most, maybe even all, medicines have been extracted from wild plants, shrubs and trees – and no doubt there are more to be discovered (note to palm oil companies and loggers: please don't chop down the rainforest). But nevertheless, there is surely no doubt that many so-called natural remedies must have been quackery or pure guesswork, and very risky. Imagine the medicinal plant explorer already with glazed eyes and a headache from searching through fields full of flowers. He's thinking: 'I'll get some hawkweed for my eyes, and I bet there is a plant growing here that would cure my headache. But which? Okay I shall take a chance on that one.'

So he nibbles it like a rabbit, washes it down with a swig from his hip flask, and feels better. Then half an hour later: 'Oh dear… I think I have poisoned myself. Oh well, you can't win 'em all.' And another one bites the dust. It is surely a candidate for one of the dodgiest jobs of the 18th century – a plant-tester for an apothecary.

But I Digress

Time to get ourselves back to the garden (thanks Joni), but not before I thank Nick at Hauxley, who got me into flowers, not by teaching me a whole list of names that I wouldn't remember, but by showing me how to look and how to appreciate the variety, intricacy and beauty of what I was seeing. From that day on for the next four or five years I always carried a camera (this was pre-mobiles) and photographed every flower that I didn't recognise. I collected the images into albums and labelled them with details of their names and habitats. It provided me with a way to pass time when, for example, I was stranded at Bristol Parkway station and snapped five new species growing around the car park. Or times when the birding was as slow as the train I was waiting for. I particularly enjoyed sorting out a collage of species from distinct areas. Nick was also my guide in Teesdale, where I first heard mention of 'limestone intrusions' and 'unimproved hay meadows,' and made acquaintance with such ingeniously named flowers as Hoary Rock-rose, Lady's Mantle, Melancholy Thistle, Moonwort and so on. No doubt every one of them was reputed to have medicinal or even magical powers. My flower photography has waned I think, mainly because the profusion and technical excellence of images on the Internet has made my activities seem somehow redundant. I do, however, still have five large albums from my first five years of botanical awareness. Browsing through them for this book brought back memories of flowers, faces and places and, even though I say it myself, some of the displays are really lovely to look at. The only negative – an apt word – was to think of all the hundreds of films I got through and how many shots I threw away. Those were the days. That's what we did before digital.

Bringing the Chilterns
to Hampstead

I have already accepted responsibility for the weird areas in my garden. Who could forget the Magic Tree, Spooky Corner, and of course Gnome Corner? Weird, intriguing, imaginative or ludicrous they may be, but even to me they are of course merely substitutes for natural landscapes. The size of my garden – pretty small – means the best I can aspire to are mini-habitats. The first thing I created was what I exaggeratingly called a 'marsh garden.' I dug a hole, put in a small chunk of butyl liner, then shoveled back the earth and assumed that rainfall would create a patch of mud which in turn would sustain bog-loving plants. In fact, the only two species that have flourished are a considerable clump of Meadowsweet with its frothy cream flowers, which is offset by a veritable golden bouquet of St John's Wort. Between them they reputedly combat bad odours and depression.

My next burst of creativity was more ambitious. By this time I had achieved the transition from the world of wacky comedy to the infinitely more dignified ethos of the BBC's Natural History Unit. Over the course of several series I visited and enthused over various regions of Britain. Many's the time I considered how I might be able to transfer more 'samples' of particular favourite landscapes back to Hampstead. I loved the limestone pavement of the Burren in Co. Clare, but it wouldn't fit in my garden any more than the snowy slopes of the Cairngorms or the Machair of the Outer Hebrides. My favourite of all was, and still is, chalk downland. For a start everything growing there is scaled down. The flowers are tiny, for example Eyebright (another optician's friend?), Milkwort, Wild Thyme and Marjoram. To truly appreciate them you have to crawl around on your hands and knees, and whilst you're down there you share the world with crickets, grasshoppers and various specialist butterflies such as Marbled Whites and Chalkhill Blues. You will even get to admire thistles, despite keep putting your hand on them. If it is natural mindfulness you seek, I really recommend gazing into the grass on a sunny day on a chalk downland and noticing every little detail of every little thing that grows and glows. If only I could I take it home.

Was it a coincidence, or a moment of déjà vu? Or a sign? Think back with me to my backyard in Rochdale in the 1940s. No lawn, no flowerbeds, just two white porcelain sinks, used for nothing. Flash forward to Hampstead in the 1980s and my new garden. And what were the only objects left by the previous owners? Two white porcelain sinks. White. The colour of chalk. This was surely a sign, and a challenge. I decided to create not one but a brace of miniature chalk downs. Years ago there was a comedy gardener on radio (Arthur Fallowfield, played by Kenneth Williams) whose catchphrase was 'The answer lies in the soil.' I used to think it was funny because he never said anything else, whatever the subject. However, when it came to gardening I suspected that he was probably right. I knew nothing about soil. Acid and alkaline were things we'd learnt about in school chemistry. You dipped litmus paper in a jar and it went red or blue. I can't even remember which was which. Or why it was so important. Was it an early version of a pregnancy test? I don't think so. The teacher certainly never mentioned gardening.

I did know that the Hampstead soil was clay, which is good for growing almost nothing, and that to create chalky soil would require the gardening equivalent of a master chef. At the garden centre I did my usual thing of *not* asking for assistance. I suppose it is similar cussedness that men have of not asking the way. It's a bit more intrepid to find it yourself, even if it means driving around for hours totally lost. If you do stop and ask, and are instantly directed to the correct destination, your response is not so much gratitude as humiliation. In much the same way, whatever you are looking for at a garden centre you want to find it yourself. It may take ages, but that's another part of the enjoyment. I believe that garden centres nowadays compensate for the demise of record shops, where I for one would browse the new releases for hours. I didn't even mind when they stopped letting you hear a few sample tracks. I enjoyed the gamble of 'playing blind' when I got the record home. Some were great and some were a huge disappointment. It is much the same with buying plants.

Some plants flourish, others wither and die. What I never do is ask for 'expert advice' and I certainly had no intention of asking a recent school-leaver on work experience: 'How do I make a chalk downland in a sink?' Instead I browsed the shelves of what appeared to be the soil improvement section, with bottles, bags and boxes of what sounded like ingredients for Harry Potter's latest spell: bone meal, pig's blood, organic chicken manure, pure screened wormcasts, bentonite powder, vilmorin, zeolite, mushroom spores, and so on. I experienced much the same feeling of confusion as when I peruse endless shelves of alternative medicines at our local health shop. I have never even heard of most of them, and I don't believe any of them work. I suspected that it could well be the same with 'medicine' for plants, but I kept searching until I finally spotted the word 'chalk' alongside other labels with C-words like calcareous and calcium. There was also lime, presumably as in limestone pavement, which is another of my favourite botanical habitats.

I don't recall what I finally bought, and I certainly don't remember what proportions I mixed together in my porcelain sink. Neither do I remember whether I planted seedlings, or grown flowers, or whether I scattered a packet of chalk-loving wildflower seed mix. What I do know is that my diminutive downland is still a happy home to harebells, pinks, knapweed and a profusion of betony. It is hardly the South Downs, but it's not a bad attempt, especially after I added a few extra touches, namely a plastic Peter Pan, three fairies and a dragon.

Enough About Gardening

I made it clear in the very first paragraph that this was not a book about how to make your garden wildlife friendly. Nevertheless, please do not assume that my garden is wildlife unfriendly. However, at first glance, it may appear to be positively hostile. A veritable deterrent to wild creatures, and especially to birds. It is as if it has been designed as one big bird scarer. For a start it is almost perpetually noisy due to the tinkling, ringing, clanking and rattling of well over a dozen wind chimes, some as diminutive and delicate as a fairy's doorbell, others with pipes as massive as those on the organ at the Royal Albert Hall. They make the sort of sonorous sounds that are normally produced by half-naked oily-chested men in colourful nappies belting huge gongs with hammers. Now if such a musician were to appear in my garden, I guarantee that all the birds would flee instantly, but whilst it is only the music of the wind they take no notice and carry on flitting and feeding. Wind chimes are presumably accepted as natural sounds and signal no threat. It is humans they are wary of.

But what about natural and unnatural sights? I have heard, read and been told that it is utterly anathema to wildlife to have mirrors in a garden. The theory is, I believe, that birds will mistake their own reflections for rivals, and will either fly away or literally attack the image in the mirror, thus risking bending their beaks, ruffling their feathers, or exhausting themselves. Were this a common problem I should have to plead guilty to intentional prolonged cruelty, or at least to willfully teasing titmice. For many years I have had five or six large mirrors hanging on various fences. Plus another dozen smaller ones and maybe 20 or 30 small fragments and slivers of glass placed amongst rockeries and wedged on tree trunks. Most of the slivers were the result of dropping a big mirror which I was trying and failing to fix in an awkward spot.

So are the birds in my garden living in a kaleidoscopic torment of their own reflections? My many years of observation suggest not. I can honestly say that on only three or four occasions have I witnessed a bird apparently bamboozled by a mirror. One was a Robin that looked as if it were admiring itself. The others were Dunnocks which, as any birdwatcher will confirm, are famous for getting in a right tizz when they see their reflection, be it in a kitchen window, or a car wing-mirror, or one of the mirrors in my garden. In fact, it was the noise of pecking that first attracted my attention. I peered into a nearby tree expecting to see a woodpecker or even a Nuthatch, until my eye was distracted by fluttering at ground-level, and there was a Dunnock jabbing like a fast-fisted boxer at an opponent who of course was jabbing back in perfect synchronicity.

I presumed it was a male, although even Dunnocks themselves seem rather confused about their sexuality and are prone to rather random promiscuity. I also witnessed the moment when at last he figured out that he was the victim of some kind of visual hoax, and he logically hopped behind the mirror in case his rival was hiding there. Which of course he wasn't. So where had he gone? Our hero hopped back out front and there was the scoundrel back in the mirror. My Dunnock tried playing 'peepo' a couple more times and finally gave up, hopping away with the Dunnock equivalent of a shrug, presumably thinking: 'I've got to admit I don't know how it's done. Never mind. I'm gonna go and see if I can find a threesome.' Which, by the way, is a favourite Dunnock activity.

So, I feel no guilt about having mirrors in my garden. No birds have been knowingly hurt or damaged by them. A few might have been at bit confused, but they might even have enjoyed it – the avian equivalent of the 'Hall of Distorting Mirrors' at a funfair (do they have them any more?). Apart from which, strategically placed mirrors can make a garden look much bigger and greener and, well, more interesting. Mirrors won't scare birds away. However, there are some things you can put in your garden which will scare the birds. At least, that is what they are meant to do.

I am sure most of us have seen a bird scarer, and even mistaken one for a live bird. Airfields – attempting to keep the runways clear of gulls or geese – often resort to placing a very realistic plastic Great Horned Owl on a nearby roof or telegraph pole. These are commonest in America, which isn't surprising because Great Horned Owl has never been recorded in Britain. If one did turn up it wouldn't be just gulls they'd have to chase off the runways. Air-traffic control tends to discourage packs of over-excited twitchers.

Mind you, I should warn you that model Great Horned Owls seems to be proliferating on this side of the Atlantic, particularly at sports grounds. What's more, they are evolving, and becoming slightly more realistic, especially those that have swiveling heads. My most recent sighting was of one perched on the roof of the pavilion during a test match at Lord's Cricket Ground. Its head movements were controlled by a man with a remote control. It was meant to keep the birds off the wicket, but the commentator gleefully pointed out a pair of pigeons that were strutting around at silly mid-on, barely a couple of metres from the stumps. Back to the drawing board? What odds on a drone owl zooming around over the pitch?

Worldwide the Peregrine Falcon is definitely the plastic predator of choice, whether it be to guard airfields and reservoirs, to keep pigeons out of Trafalgar Square, or too discourage egrets and herons from gorging themselves at fish farms. Rather curiously, full-size plastic herons are also placed along the shores of fish ponds, and indeed garden ponds, to prevent fish – gold, ornamental or edible – from being snaffled by… real herons. Which brings me to a not infrequently heard complaint about bird scarers: they may look like the real thing – almost – but they don't work.

In the case of the garden pond goldfish-guarding heron it isn't surprising. Imagine if you will that you have purchased your immaculately accurate model Grey Heron. You have rather undignifyingly stuck its fixing pole up its vent, and carefully positioned it on the pond shoreline, leaning slightly forward, with dagger-like beak poised as if about to spear one of your prized goldfish, carp or whatever. At which moment, up in the sky above a real live heron is drifting over the neighbourhood in search of a promising fish pond. Eventually, the glint of water catches his eye. He also sees what is undeniably another Grey Heron, seemingly engaged in successful fishing.

So, does our real heron think: 'Oh damn. He's beaten me to it. That pond ain't big enough for both of us.' And away he flies, leaving the garden owner assuring himself that thirty quid's worth of fake heron was money well spent.

Or does the real heron look down and think: 'Ah, there's one of my mates stalking in the shallows, there must be fish in that pond. I shall drop down and join him. Should be enough for two.' Imagine his delight as he gobbles up the lot, and the plastic rival doesn't even compete.

Wildfowlers used to, and no doubt still do, use decoys. They put out accurate model birds – plastic or wood, moulded or sculpted – for the very reason that wild birds will be attracted to join them, and thus be easier to shoot. The survivors would of course then fly off, but it would be the men and the shotguns that scared them, not the decoys. The ducks thought they were their friends.

You will have deduced by now that I am insinuating that these plastic predators really don't work. Correct. Moreover, they are ineffective not just by the fish pond, but also in the rest of the garden. Why else would I have so many of them in mine? Okay this isn't a book about attracting birds, but neither is it about frightening them away. I have a simple theory about birds. They are not stupid. Moreover, they are totally aware of whether or not a creature – especially another bird – is alive or dead, or rather real or fake. Why else would I be able to fix a totally accurate model Peregrine, with all the correct markings and colours, and even with a trickle of red on its recently blooded talons, on the corner of the green roof on my garden shed. I lurked on the other side of the garden with camera in hand, ready to record how long it would take for any garden birds to approach one of its most fearsome enemies. I didn't have to wait long. In less than ten minutes there were four Woodpigeons strutting round the raptor, and within another minutes there was a Robin perched on its head. Seeing that instigated a challenge that is ongoing – I try to get pictures of every species in my garden, perched on top of a creature that it would otherwise steer clear of.

When I say 'creature' am I implying not just birds? I am indeed. In fact at this point it behoves me to present an inventory of non-real wildlife that resides in my garden. Some of the species are quite logical, others are certainly not. No creature is banned, but there is one criterion – they must be realistic. Accurate in shape, posture and colours. In a word, lifelike. I mention this to emphasise that if you shop around, either at garden centres or online, there are some really good 'models' out there. There are also some – in fact more – very very bad ones. A few of these may be intentionally bad taste, however the majority are probably just bad. Misshapen, with silly expressions on their faces, or wearing inappropriate clothes. To be honest, I consider any clothes worn by any bird or animal to be inappropriate. Even if it isn't real. I wouldn't actually ban twee garden creatures entirely, but I do think they should be displayed in sections marked: lifelike, intentionally naff, ironical, embarrassingly incompetent, and cringingly twee.

I am by no means claiming that every figure in my garden falls into the 'tastefully lifelike' category. Gnome Corner is surely proof of that. As are the discreetly placed fairies and dragons. But I do make sure they know their place. Call it segregation if you like, but personally I believe that realism and fantasy do not mix.

Here then is a more or less complete inventory of my fake but realistic wildlife.

Peregrine Falcon and Gyr Falcon. The latter is actually a Peregrine that I painted white and to which I added some darker vermiculations – this task required some delicate brushwork.

Kestrel. Dangling from a fishing line on the 'Magic Tree' to give the illusion of flight. It is rarely convincing because it tends to turn upside-down. The original plumage details have deteriorated, but I have touched it up, as it were.

Great Horned Owl. A favourite perch for Robins, Wrens and tits.

Owl sp. This started off as a Great Horned, but I sawed off the 'ears,' painted it grey, and mobbed it with model tits, robins, wrens, two chipmunks, a squirrel, and so on. I'm still not sure what species the owl is though.

Little Owls. I have at least six, but they are well-suited to perching and peeping and are consequently not at all obvious.

Herons. I actually started with two common Grey Herons, but I have transformed them both. One is now a Purple Heron, which was tricky to paint. The other was a Great White Egret, which wasn't. There is also a very nice Grey Heron peering from behind a palm tree, but it is curiously only about half life-size.

This rather confuses the issue of people telling me: 'Bill, I saw this huge heron over London today.'

To which I gently but pedantically inform them: 'It was not huge, it was heron-sized.' They are all the same size. Which is indeed huge. Except for the half-size one in my garden.

Glossy Ibis. Another of my transformations. It started as a Curlew. It wasn't easy to mix the right maroony-goldy colour, but since it is almost hidden by reeds and irises it doesn't really matter.

White Stork and nest. I am rather proud of this one. It is fully life-size and it is perched about eight feet up in a willow tree, on a nest I made myself with twigs and all manner of detritus as storks are wont to do. What I would really like is a chick or two in the nest. The nearest I have come so far is to use an RSPB Oystercatcher, which has at least got the right colours of black and white, with a red beak. It wasn't a success, as next morning it had been ejected from the nest. I'd like to think that it was the stork protesting – this is *not* my baby – but I suspected a Jay or a Magpie. Every year I freshen up the stork's white plumage (they never are really white, are they?) and check its beak, which originally kept falling off, but is now firmly fixed with a dollop of chewing gum.

Wildfowl. As behoves the progenitors of decoys, there is quite a variety of ducks. These include three Mallards (two males), Pintail, Teal, Wigeon, Pochard and Tufted Duck. Most of those were originally capable of floating, but eventually there always came a morning when they sprang a leak and keeled over. When that happens I relocate them onto a bank or onto rocks. There is also a male

Long-tailed Duck and a female Harlequin Duck. Incidentally, I didn't get the Harlequin from a garden centre. In fact, I found it in the shed. It wasn't a Harlequin then. It was so old and manky that I couldn't identify it, so I painted it blackish and dabbed a few white patches onto its face. Easy! Maybe some day I will try to create a male. I have already created a female Wood Duck who is courted by three males.

Thrushes. Another feature I am rather proud of is my collection of rare thrushes. None of them are still in their original state. In fact most of them started off as Starlings. Then one sunny Sunday I sat at my garden table with a selection of little paint pots and appropriate brushes and transformed the ancient Starlings into four Redwings, a Fieldfare, a Ring Ouzel, an Eyebrowed Thrush, a Dusky Thrush, a Black-throated Thrush, a Red-throated Thrush and an American Robin. And just to acknowledge their origins I did a Rose-coloured Starling too. There's also an American Red-winged Blackbird, which is in a different family altogether, albeit rather thrush-shaped.

Other Passerines. As you might expect, there are lots and lots of little birds. I have four Blue Tits, two Great Tits, two Wrens, a Song Thrush, a Blackbird, two Swallows perched and two more feeding chicks in nests, quite a few Robins (but not as many as there are real ones) of varying sizes. The biggest Robin is the size of a swan and was once an RSPB collecting box. I don't think I stole it, so how did it get there?

Kingfishers. Two Common Kingfishers, both perched, and one White-breasted Kingfisher – well it is now that I have added the white breast. What it was originally or where it came from I have no idea. The same goes for a pair of small green kingfishers that I have yet to find in any field guide.

Woodpeckers. A precarious challenge to the ageing gardener such as I, which gets tougher every year, is to risk climbing up ladders or even hanging on branches in order to fix woodpeckers in the right places. America is represented by a Red-headed Woodpecker and two Williamson's Sapsuckers. Britain by a single Great Spotted Woodpecker, which I fastened to a tree stump close to the back door feeders, where it often shares space with the live version of its kind. They take no notice of each other.

Miscellaneous other birds. I'm nearly through the birds. There is one male Pheasant, one of the few that nobody has shot at yet. And talking of shooting, I have at least seven Turtle Doves perched around my garden. They do not appear to migrate, which is no doubt how they manage to survive. 'Malta? No thanks, I'll stick to Hampstead.'

Any more? Magpie. Male and female Golden Oriole, which are again ex-Starlings. I was particularly proud of the female. I mean anyone can slap on black and gold, but subtle olive, shading to pale yellow with a touch of grey – that's art. And to round off there are Goldfinch, Greenfinch, Wood Thrush and Ruby-throated Hummingbird. Who knows what's to come next?

At a rough count I have at least 120 fake birds in my garden. I have no evidence whatsoever to suggest that they scare away, deter, or even bewilder any of the real birds (much more about them in later chapters).

It is, however, conspicuously evident that the models provide an endless miscellany of perches. Whether or not the birds enjoy this, I do not know, but I do know that I certainly do. They have provided hours of fun for me and my camera.

But wait. I do not simply specialise in counterfeit birds. My garden is a fine example of counterfeit biodiversity. Animals, insects, amphibians and more are all there somewhere. Don't worry, this list is shorter, but not much.

It is probably easiest to list these under headings or habitats. There is a sort of logic applied but it is not as pedantic or purist as with the birds. For example, size is not necessarily the same as in life. This is best illustrated by the small Jurassic-themed raised flowerbed, which is home to three different species of dinosaur, none of them bigger than a mouse, They share the space with a miniature elephant family, a leopard, a bear, a rhino, and an extremely realistic gorilla which is far from life-size but is at least a hundred times the size of the *Tyrannosaurus rex*. It is also arguably the most perched on creature in the garden. It is rarely without a Robin, a Blackbird or a Great Tit on its head and it is steadily developing a white fringe from their droppings. Nevertheless, true to his kind, my gorilla is forever smiling.

Every one of the five little ponds has something appropriate lounging on its banks, wallowing in the shallows, or even floating free. There are rubber frogs and pairs of both European Otters and Sea Otters. Crocodiles, alligators, a single Gharial, two tiny turtles and a medium-sized tortoise. The pebbly shore of the top pond has assorted crustaceans stranded on the beach and a rubber octopus with most of its tentacles dangling in the water, whilst counterfeit dragonflies, butterflies and bugs abound, which is just as well because there have been precious few of the real insects in recent years. The shallow corner of the top pond is the favourite bathing place of my concrete hippopotamus. It is not actually a whole hippo, just the head. Well half the head really. The ears, eyes and nostrils protrude just above the surface. The rest of the animal is underwater, propped up by two house bricks. If I ever have to adjust the pond's aerating pump there is a definite risk of crushing my fingers.

Imagine going to A&E and they'd ask: 'So, what did that then?'

'A Hippo!'

Farm animals are represented by three little pigs (not nursery rhyme types wearing dungarees) and two lambs grazing on the lawn. There are family groups of fake foxes and equally fake cubs, a pair of deer with attendant bambi, and half a dozen semi-subterranean moles, one of which has been sprayed white so that he qualifies as doorkeeper to Spooky Corner (remember that?). There are of course plenty of badgers. There may well be seven or eight, but I often forget where I put them, and – just like in nature – they are shy, elusive and rarely seen. In fact, I am assuming they are still there somewhere. Maybe they have been culled. If so I shall sue the government.

And that is the end of the inventory. Over 150 counterfeit creatures. I may have missed a few – scorpions, snakes, Wood Mice, chipmunks, raccoon, guinea pig, and both Red and Grey Squirrels nibbling on the same branch. Oh yes, and one of my all time favourites, a full-size Wild Boar. Or rather what's left of it.

The boar was a birthday present from my fine friend Marek, who is one of the great naturalists of Poland. Every year he drives across Europe to attend the annual Birdfair at Rutland Water. There was just room in his van for his promotional material, his family, and my present: the plastic boar, accompanied by a portly bearded fellow dressed all in green and with binoculars around his neck. Frankly it could have resembled either of us, except for the flaw that one hand was missing. Marek apologised profusely, and duly blamed the German customs who had been less than gentle at the border. I naturally assured him that the green man's disability in no way diminished the splendour of the gift, and I duly installed it in my garden under a lilac tree close to one of the bird-feeding areas.

One morning the whimsical notion struck me that I could provide the green man with an artificial hand. This I did by stuffing a gardening glove with waste paper and squeezing it into the broken wrist. As I was adjusting the hand – a delicate operation – it struck me that the break was rather cleaner than what you would expect from a clumsy German customs guard. It was as if the hand had been intentionally severed, perhaps because it had been holding something undesirable? A bag full of narcotics simply wasn't Marek's style. Perhaps the green man had been brandishing a dead gamebird? Or a rabbit? Or... of course. To quote Basil Fawlty, the answer was 'The bleedin' obvious!' The green man was a hunter. He had been holding a gun. Marek would not offend me by even mentioning hunting, and had duly made sure that the green man would never kill again by snapping off his rifle. I am sure that Marek would be delighted that whilst the boar has long since been ravaged by wear and tear, the green man still stands proudly under the lilac tree, now leaning on a walking stick provided by me, and – what's more – he looks perpetually delighted to watch the comings and goings of all the garden birds, even if some of them occasionally poop on his smart green hat, which I repaint at least once a year.

So that's it, a full list of the fake, model, plastic, plaster, resin – call them what you will – creatures that I have put in my garden. Some of them will be featured in other stories in this book and others you will recognise from photos. Before that however, let me just assure you that there will be absolutely definitely no mention or depiction whatsoever of Meerkats. Either singly or in groups of four, whether unclothed or wearing costumes, and certainly not doing impersonations of historical figures and rock stars. I recently did some research on this inexplicable phenomenon and discovered that you can purchase Meerkats dressed as Elvis Presley, Dolly Parton, Freddie Mercury and Bob Dylan – I bet he's flattered. That's no way to treat a Nobel prize-winner. I also found Shakespeare, Charlie Chaplin, Sherlock Holmes, James Bond, Henry VIII, Robin Hood and Lawrence of Arabia, as well as a Beefeater, an astronaut, a judge, and a Coldstream Guard wearing a bearskin hat. Surely it is grossly inappropriate for a furry animal to wear another furry animal? There are also Meerkats riding miniature vehicles, including a bike, a car and a Lambretta. Plus a golfer and a bagpiper. From what I have seen so far – and I intend to avoid ever seeing a another Meerkat for the rest of my life unless it is in the wild – the oddest Meerkat character you can purchase to jolly up your garden is dressed as a tin-hatted British footsoldier from the First World War. Some sort of tribute I suppose, but why? I have heard of the Desert Rats, but not the Desert Meerkats. Anyway, no harm done I suppose. Mind you, I am not sure I approve of the Meerkat that is a dead ringer for Hitler. Where will it end? Who knows, but I wish it would.

At this point, I suppose it would be understandable if a fanatical Meerkat-collector accused me of being equally obsessed with gnomes. Certainly I cannot deny that by no means all of them are in traditional gnome costumes. I have various sporting gnomes in appropriate gear, including footballers, golfers, cricketers, a shot-putter and, I admit, a disproportionate number of fishermen. There are also several musicians and singers playing to a sleeping audience. Plus there are plenty of gnome-sized gardeners brandishing their tools. Which reminds me, I assure you that I do not now – and never have – owned any pornographic gnomes, although I am assured that they do exist, even though – as far as I know – female gnomes do not! I leave you to draw your own conclusions. If we were pitting gnomes against Meerkats, costume-wise they'd come out pretty equal. However, where the gnomes have it is in their almost infinite variety of shapes, sizes and facial expressions, whilst – let's own up – Meerkats all look the same. I rest my case.

Tails from a Ludicrous Garden

At this point I feel I should reiterate my warning, or my promise, that this book is not about attracting birds or any other wildlife to your garden. If you want one of those, there are shelves full of them in the bookshops. They vary, but frankly not much. None of them will recommend plastic predators and resin raptors, nor broken mirrors, and definitely not gnomes (well not more than a few). I would like to think that they don't recommend Meerkats in fancy dress either. One thing that many authors will suggest is that you keep a list of the birds seen in, from or over your garden. I agree with that. So much so that I have been doing it myself ever since I moved into the house by Hampstead Heath. It is all memories now but some of them are quite impressive. A Greenshank flying past my bedroom window. Four Bewick's Swans in a snowstorm. A Woodcock on the doorstep (a window kill), and passage migrants in spring and autumn, in numbers that I feel sure were far more numerous than they are nowadays. Sedge and Reed Warblers, Redstarts, Pied and Spotted Flycatchers, and a Wood Warbler joining in the dawn chorus.

The extraordinary thing is that I lived there for several years without ever venturing far onto the heath itself. Doesn't take much deduction does it? If I got so many birds in the garden, there must be a lot more out on the heath. There were. And sometimes there still are. But – here's a funny thing – from the pond-side path I can see across to my old house and the garden and the nearby trees, but I have never spotted anything good there in recent years. Maybe it's the constant cacophony of house 'improvements,' loft conversions, basement extensions, pneumatic drills, clanking scaffolding and bellowing builders that has put them off. The House Martin colony has gone too.

Naturally I still keep a list, and every now and again I get a 'garden tick' as birders say, although personally I find it slightly demeaning for a bird that is after all a rarity in the context. Surely it deserves a more dignified title. How about a 'garden goody'? As the years have passed the 'goodies' have slowly proliferated. I no longer live on the shores of Hampstead pond, but I still have a sky. I include birds seen flying over and if I heard a call I was sure of I would count it, even if I never saw the bird. I mean, who cares except me? My garden, my rules.

My full garden list is at the very end of the book. It's not exactly mind-boggling, but if you are consumed with curiosity by all means flick forward. Do come back though, as I have some science for you. Really? Well sort of.

The Home of Discoveries

Long before *Springwatch* I came up with the idea for a programme about the everyday lives of the garden birds in a small English village. I described it as 'an avian soap opera,' and suggested the title of *Rookside*. It was rejected, but then most things are. I sometimes wonder if the public realise just how stressful, upsetting and often humiliating life is if you are what is called 'creative.' You could be a writer of books or TV scripts, an actor or actress, a singer-songwriter, a dancer, an artist, and so on. Whatever you create you have to sell, even though there may be no obvious practical demand for it. It would be hard to insist that you are providing an essential service. Moreover, and perhaps most painfully, you are constantly being judged. I personally decided to abandon a very brief acting career because I found auditions utterly unbearable. A voice in the dark announcing 'We'll let you know,' or even just 'Next,' is demeaning once or twice, but time after time it becomes ghastly and dispiriting. I know everyone's life –

and career – has its ups and downs, but the creative road may be the only one where you can be certain you will experience a lot more downs than ups. Personally, I admit I have been very very lucky to have co-operated with the right people on the right ideas. In this context, the right ideas simply means the ones you were lucky enough to sell, which usually also involves knowing the right people.

Please forgive what might be verging on a rant. I am not pleading sympathy for out-of-work actors, or unpublished authors, or penniless artists – even though they may well deserve it – nor am I whingeing about my own relative paucity of employment in the medium I worked in on and off for 50 years. So what am I on about? I reckon it is writing about my garden that has set me thinking. I was thinking about that *Rookside* idea. It was inspired by two things. One was a book published in 1952 called *Birds as Individuals* by Len Howard, which was based on the author's observations of the regular avian visitors to her garden. The second element was my own garden. I too gave some of the regular birds names, and kept a diary of the highs and especially the lows of what I regarded as 'my birds.' Individuals yes, but mine.

Len Howard lived alone in a cottage in Suffolk. She probably wouldn't have called herself a birdwatcher or an ornithologist, but she was most definitely a bird lover, and a meticulous observer. Her conviction – as is clear from the title of her book – was that birds have differing characteristics, looks, behaviour, and even what one might call personalities. Perhaps not as obvious or as varied as in human beings, but certainly far more than most scientists would accept. Indeed, I suspect that most scientists were indulgent rather than excited by Ms Howard's theories. I suppose one might argue that such an obsessively pursued thesis tells us as much about human behaviour as birds. One thing is clear, which is that Len Howard's writings were both intriguing and entertaining enough to impress the wildlife stars of their day. Aldous Huxley contributed a foreword and Eric Hosking a portfolio of delightful photos. *Birds as Individuals* probably irked the purists, but it also steered a path towards Johnny Morris and, dare I say, even myself. One of the BBC's early precursors of *Springwatch* was *Bird In the Nest*, which brought live action from inside the nests of mostly garden birds. The shows were presented by the RSPB's Peter Holden and myself. The real stars were of course the various individual birds and their families. Almost inevitably, the most popular characters were Blue Tits, Great Tits and Robins. The differences between this series and the more, may I say, traditional BBC Natural History programmes were that invariably the individuals were given names, and that they were attributed with emotions, feelings and personalities. I wonder if Len Howard got a credit, or maybe even a royalty?

The species that is most featured in Ms Howard's book is the Great Tit. Well not just *the* Great Tit, or *a* Great Tit, but lots and lots of them. Watching them was the equivalent of her being invited into their house and in turn they were invited into hers. There are photos of them perched on her shoulder, or on her typewriter or the piano. She didn't teach them to play, nor to sing particular songs, though she did claim to be able to recognise a number of individual birds by their distinctive phrases. An achievement indeed, considering that Great Tits are infamous for making all sorts of noises, hence the old adage: 'If you don't recognise the song, it's a Great Tit.'

To which Ms Howard would probably reply: 'Which Great Tit?' She gave every one of them a name. And of course spoke to them accordingly.

Any one of us – and that includes me – who feels a bit bashful about talking to garden birds, need no longer be inhibited. Amongst the Great Tit names in Len Howard's garden were Puggy, Teaser, Buffer, Inkey, Dimple, Curly, Whiskers (shouldn't that be a cat?), Baldhead, Fatty and Star. And many many more, all accurately assigned to their places in their family trees. She claimed to be able to recognise last year's offspring, despite them having moulted. Newcomers were at first given 'literal' names such as the 'Back Wall Stranger,' but if they settled in they would soon be duly baptised. She must have had quite a memory. She records one particular day when she reckoned there were 60 Great Tits in her little Suffolk garden. And she knew them all. Put 60 of my close friends in my garden, and I'd be pushed to remember a couple of dozen names. Actually I doubt that I have 60 friends.

I admit I am not sure if Len Howard's Great Tits truly proved that birds are individuals beyond some basic variations, but I do know that I was thoroughly intrigued when I read her book. It was published 1952, when I was 11.

I also know that when I finally acquired a proper garden of my own, complete with nest boxes and feeders and a selection of garden birds, it wasn't long before I had given them all names, and held conversations with them, and was keeping an eye on what was going on in their lives. I also know that the first drama I witnessed involved a family of Great Tits.

The Greatest Tits

I have put up at least half a dozen nest boxes around my garden. They are meant to provide a variety of choices, and also to save the garden birds energy, because they don't have to spend ages searching for suitable holes and collect nesting material. Instead they can get on with the mating, egg-laying, incubating and eventually chick-feeding, which is of course the bit they really need energy for. Occupying a nest box made to proper stipulations and dimensions, especially with the correct hole-size, should also be safer from egg- and chick-snafflers such as squirrels, rats, Jays, cats and the like. However, like many before me it was several years before anything occupied one of my nest boxes. I did have birds nesting in the garden, but almost perversely just about anywhere else but in a box. I had Blue Tits up a drainpipe, Robins in the guttering, Blackbirds on an ivy-covered fencepost, and Wrens inside a garden ornament labeled 'Goblins' Castle.'

Then finally, one spring, at last I noticed a lot of coming and going outside the classy wooden nest box I had fixed on a 'ship lap' wall amongst the branches of a lilac tree. I had chosen the site carefully. Lilac branches are very thin and unstable. They are great perches for birds, but too weak and flimsy for squirrels, rats and cats. The box was well sheltered from the sun and finally – an aesthetic touch – I imagine the view from the nest of lilac blossoms with the occasional Red Admiral or Holly Blue butterfly would be delightfully idyllic.

Any of you who have observed an occupied nest box will agree that it isn't obvious what's happening in there. I have, on more than one occasion, been unsure if there is laying or incubation going on inside, only to suddenly be surprised by a frantic burst of coming and going, which indicates that the eggs have hatched. Even this isn't always obvious until after a few days when you begin to hear the chicks squeaking with excitement as soon as a parent comes back with food. It is an anxious time for the tit family, and it was an anxious time for me. This was of course during the fallow years between *Bird in the Nest* finishing and *Springwatch* starting. Of course now you can buy a nest box with built in closed-circuit camera and microphone, and if you like the idea of having a real-life natural history presenter, I am not expensive.

Meanwhile, in that challenging pre-digital era, the only clue to my Great Tits' well-being was to stand in the garden at a discreet distance, and look and listen. Which is what I had been doing for half an hour one weekend morning before becoming increasingly anxious that something wasn't right. An adult came and went and chicks duly squeaked, but the gap between visits seemed a little longer than yesterday.

Me with my pet owl.

Right: My much-loved present from Marek.

Opposite above: You never see a female gnome.

Opposite below: Gnome corner. No vacancies.

Below: Mole, gnome and gorilla practising their song and dance routine.

Jay, about to drop an acorn down next door's chimney

Right: Wren showing off its translucent wings.

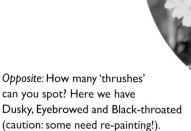

Opposite: How many 'thrushes' can you spot? Here we have Dusky, Eyebrowed and Black-throated (caution: some need re-painting!).

Spooky corner.

It's true, Toads *do* need help crossing the road.

He's behind you, Mr Robin!

Above left:
Even baby
rats can
climb.

Above right: The
cutest baby rat
you ever did see.

Above centre: Mouse attempting to beat the 'how many
mealworms can you eat in an hour' record. Only open to mice.

Below: How did five rats get in a bird feeder? How do they get out?

Spot the dog.

Lapwings, just like
I saw them when I
was a boy.

Fantastic view from up here.

The annual embarrassing
moult. 'I know I haven't
got a tail.'

Dunnock perched on Purple Heron – a frequent sight in my garden.

Storks nest. A lot of work.
I should know – I built it.

Looking petrified by
a giant Great Tit.

Above: Ooops. Wren losing its balance, nearly.
Below left: Gyr Falcon, originally a Peregrine.
I recommend Weathershield White.
Below right: Peregrine scaring off all the
other birds. Not!

Above left: Lime Hawk-Moth.
Above right: Jersey Tiger. One of the few garden creatures that have become more common in London.
Below: Wow. Cop the feathers on that! It's a Feathered Thorn moth.

Above: Lime Hawk-Moth admiring its portrait in the field guide.
Opposite inset: Poplar Hawk-Moth. Another success for the moth trap.
Below: Red Underwing moth.

Welcome to the Jay disco
– complete with glitterball.

I began to wonder if perhaps there was only one parent. I watched an adult Great Tit come and go, but was it the same bird twice? Was it a male? Or female? Had we lost mum or dad? Mum and dad was as near I had got to naming them. Where was Len Howard when I needed her?

I feared the worst. Proof was at hand. Or rather, under my foot. To my dismay I was standing on an ex-Great Tit. I recognised the blue-tinged quill-like wing-feathers. There was also lemon fluff plucked from the body and scattered nearby. The formerly glossy black of the head was already abraded by frantically squeezing in and out of the nest box, and was now further desecrated and blood-stained. It was no consolation to know that I hadn't killed it. I hadn't witnessed the crime but I was certain of the culprit. Cat. It had waited, pounced, killed and scurried off home to its cosy cat basket and bowl of Whiskas. Leaving one less Great Tit. No, worse than that. There was a family in the box. I didn't know how many. Chances are half a dozen or more. They were now a single-parent family. Could a single parent manage to feed them? At that moment he or she hopped onto a lilac branch holding a tiny caterpillar. 'Can you do it?' I asked. 'You are on your own now, you know. How many kids are there in there? Quite a lot, but you are probably not sure yourself. Its dark and there's not much time for counting. Anyway, it won't be easy on your own, so I tell you what: I will help you.' With that promise, I gingerly removed what was left of the dead parent bird and flipped it onto the compost heap.

I was as good as my word. I admit that I wasn't up at dawn as most birds are, and I didn't go searching for caterpillars or digging for worms. I did go and get worms, but only from the shed. I can honestly say that whatever food I put out for the birds – sunflower seeds, fat balls, niger seeds, peanuts, and so on – not everything is eaten by everyone. It can vary so much that I do begin to wonder if birds are indeed individuals and some can be fussy eaters. It is widely accepted that the little black niger seeds are universally adored by Goldfinches, but not in my garden. In recent years the number of Goldfinches has gone up but the feeder full of niger hasn't gone down. It stayed at the same level for over a year until it began to sprout. I have now removed it but the Goldfinches continue to nip away at the sunflower hearts.

There is one thing I can put out that gets an instant reaction from more or less every individual of every species. Mealworms. Live mealworms. Not the dry ones, which look about as appetising as sawdust. In fact, a sculptress friend of mine packs her fragile works of art in dried mealworms in preference to cotton wool or polystyrene granules, which is appropriate, since most of her work is brilliantly realistic birds or small mammals. Maybe her customers get a little frisson of alarm before they appreciate the humour. Live mealworms would probably get less of a smile, but they'd go down well in the garden no matter what the species.

The 'caged' feeders are meant to be for little birds that can nip in and out, but I have had hours of amusement watching bigger birds flapping, fluttering and falling off, and attempting to dangle like the tits. Jays, Woodpigeons, Magpies and parakeets. Show them a mealworm and they lose all dignity. The downside, however, was that the recently widowed Great Tit was going have a lot of competition. It wasn't a long way from the nest box to the feeders and back, but it might be a flight too long. I moved a mealworm dispenser and stuck it on the window, not much more than a metre from the nest box. I had retreated only a few steps when the adult Great Tit popped his or her head out, as if it had heard me up to something out there, immediately spotted the feeder, zipped in, grabbed two mealworms and shot back into the box. Excited chattering ensued, which was presumably adolescent Great Tit language for 'Blimey that was quick.' By which time the adult was out again and back with another helping.

The routine seemed to be going well, but I was still concerned that it would be hard for a single parent to bring up a whole brood. Then one morning it became harder. I was getting the day's mealworm ration from the shed when a Great Tit landed by my shoulder and then seemed to be following me back towards the feeders. At first I assumed it was my single parent getting impatient, as I and Len Howard know they do. They sometimes even give you a 'get on with it' nip. However, I then realised that this wasn't my bird at all, or if it was something very nasty had happened to it. Its left leg was dangling, presumably broken. It was time to talk. 'How did that happen? It is you, isn't it? Are you going to be able to manage?' He or she answered that one by flitting into the nest hole with the leg dangling behind, then emerging carrying a faecal sac as if to prove that a broken leg wasn't going to disrupt any family duties. The chicks in the box chorused their appreciation.

I didn't see the youngsters actually fledge, but neither did I find any piles of feathers or smears of blood, and that summer there were young Great Tits constantly coming and going at the feeders. Unlike Len Howard, I couldn't tell one from another, and therefore I couldn't give them names. Except, of course, the heroic single-legged single parent to whom I like to think I gave a helping hand. Or rather a helping foot.

I know for sure that it survived the winter and my wife and daughter always gave this bird a name-check. That Great Tit was known to us all as 'Limpy.'

For the Man Who Has
Nearly Everything

For my 65th birthday my wife Laura bought me a very special present. A rubber toad. I already had a number of fake frogs scattered round the garden ponds and a goodly population of real ones. It always intrigued me how the annual frog gangbang that occurred over two or three damp spring nights always took place only in the pond nearest the house. I should explain that over the years the lawn has diminished as the ponds have proliferated; at the last count there were five and a half, the half being a sunken saucepan which doubles up as a drinking bowl for the birds and is an appropriate setting for a small plastic Jesus to demonstrate his 'walking on the water' trick. This is achieved, by the way, by standing him on a piece of broken glass on half a brick just below water's surface. I shall be returning to the Messiah's relationship with Great Tits in a subsequent chapter.

Meanwhile, back to amphibians. I have never ever seen a live frog in Jesus's saucepan. They do visit four other ponds, but only sporadically, and I have never witnessed mating or spawning in any of them. The fact is that 100 per cent of the frog action takes place in pond number five, which is nearest to the back door. On the face of it, this isn't all that surprising, since number five is undoubtedly the most impressive pond, whether you are a frog or not. It is a sequel to the original, which developed a leaking liner problem, whereupon I redesigned the whole site with a moulded fibreglass version. I suppose that it is really a 'fake' pond, but you wouldn't know it. I have built up the banks as mini-rockeries, upon which flourish a pleasing variety of delicate little flowers such as saxifrages and various herbs, alongside a patch of lungwort (intestinally inclined gardeners may prefer the name *Pulmonaria*) and a bouquet of Water Avens. Both plants are loved by bees. Pond weed would take over the whole pond, but once its pink spikes have gone I give it a thorough but utterly skill-less thinning out. I just stick my hand in and pull, and end up with dripping wet clothes in the process. There are also a couple of rocks and two miniature wooden bridges – just bits of wood really – which are used by baby frogs contemplating their first risky hop into the big wide world, the first challenge of which is to avoid being snapped up by the local Robin, who celebrates by having a good old splash around till he is so soggy that he needs to dry off in the sun.

All in all then, if I were a frog this is the pond I would most approve of and I would recommend it to my froggy friends. My froggy friends obviously agree. It is very popular. However, that in itself is rather odd. Frogs, like many water creatures, are generally faithful to 'traditional' breeding grounds. They do not take readily to new facilities. By this token, the frogs visiting my garden should prefer the oldest pond, but they don't. They by far prefer the newest. Of course, I take this as a compliment to my pond-designing skills. When it comes to providing ideal homes for frogs, I am clearly better than nature.

There are a couple of aquatic creatures I have yet to lure into my mini-wetlands. I have never seen a newt within the garden boundaries, despite one of my neighbours harbouring a small colony. Nor have I had a toad. I once bemoaned this deprivation in the presence of Laura. Her reaction hovered somewhere between 'Oh really?' and 'What do you expect me to do about it?'

She then added what I took to be a rather malformed joke: 'Why don't you wait until your birthday? You never know.' Of course, knowing Laura I should've known.

I can truthfully say that I have never seen such a magnificent rubber toad. Or perhaps rubber any animal. Of course a would-be model toad-maker does start with the advantage that toadskin looks like rubber anyway. Not smooth rubber, as worn by deep-sea divers or at kinky parties, but textured rubber, more like scary alien monsters in sci-fi films. I think the official adjective is 'warty'. If they really are warts, it is a hell of a condition isn't it? It almost makes you feel sorry for the monsters. Keep using the ointment.

I am being frivolous, and I shouldn't be because Laura's present was truly impressive. Totally realistic to look at, or to touch. What a birthday gift, and truly just what I wanted. I was like a kid with a kitten. Me and my toad. I even cuddled it for a few minutes, before addressing the crucial challenge of deciding where it would look best in the garden. It had to be next to, and overlooking, pool number five. Only the best for this handsome giant. Oh, I didn't tell you, it wasn't what we in Britain would call toad-sized. If you were Australian, perhaps it would be more normal. The notorious Cane Toads are pretty huge, and they spread in such numbers that they can force traffic off the Australian highways. I once saw a film of them being squashed. The sight was repulsive and the sound was worse. I never did think to look under my toad's belly in case it said 'Made in Australia,' but I suspect Hong Kong or Vietnam was more likely. When I asked Laura where she had got it, she said from the grotesquely overpriced knick-knack shop down the road. Amazing what you can find in Hampstead. I was so enamoured of my toad that I decided I should play safe and go and buy another one – an understudy, or even a mate – but alas they were sold out. I asked the overpriced shopkeeper – who was identifiable by her 'we saw you coming' badge – when were they expecting a new consignment of rubber toads. I was grieved by the reply: 'Probably never. Your wife bought the only one we have ever sold.'

I was as deflated as my toad would be if I accidentally stuck a fork in it. I really would have to be careful where I put it. And look after it.

I spent an hour redistributing fake frogs, and repositioning the resin Wood Duck family, the half-a-Mallard that looks as if it is 'dabbling up-tails all,' and the four ducklings that started off yellow but are now a wilder shade of beige because I repainted them. I created a natural frame with carefully arched miniature reeds, and finally I affectionately placed Toady – I just had to give him a personal name – with his haunches lightly lapped by the water and his bulging eyes peering through the rushes, wary of danger and yet big enough to be confident that he could be harmed by no-one or nothing.

The next morning he had gone! I was going to say he had disappeared, but that is an exaggeration because it only took half a minute or so to find him. He hadn't disappeared, he had been moved. Even with my embarrassingly vivid imagination I am under no illusions about rubber animals coming to life at night like in *Toy Story*. It's a pity they don't, but we have the major consolation that real animals do. Clearly this was exactly what had happened that night or early that morning. I assumed that the garden had not been visited by a toadnapper, an indiscriminate fake-animal thief, or even, perish the thought, a gnome burglar. However, a relieved scan told me that the only thing that wasn't in the same position as when I went to bed was the toad. He wasn't easy to spot. He was lying on his back in the middle of the lawn. No damage. No signs of a fight. I replaced him in his designated spot and placed a few more stones and a couple of oyster shells around him as if somehow they would provide protection. I was out all day, but back in the garden in the evening, and as far as I could see everything was untouched and still in place. So had it been rubber toad kinesis? A tiny tornado, or a clumsy cat? I'd wait and see what happened by next morning.

It was the same but different. Again, the toad had been moved. This time he was lying on his side on the edge of pond number two. Nobody ever goes there. But in fact he wasn't alone. Floating upside-down in the water was one of the previously yellow ducklings. I hadn't bothered to paint their bellies so it was pretty conspicuous. In the process of returning it to its Wood Duck parents, I noticed that there were a few signs of gnawing on its left cheek. It hadn't been decapitated, but it looked as if something had tried.

I admit I was beginning to have my suspicions and I feared for the safety of most of the creatures in my garden. Real or otherwise. However I also had to acknowledge that I had mixed feelings. Anyone who observes wildlife will, I am sure, have had this experience every time they are aware that a predator is around. Wildlife cameramen face it all the time. I shared it myself on the beach in Patagonia watching a baby seal lolloping on the shoreline with the fin of a Killer Whale gliding ominously in the background. I said to the camera that I was torn between fearing for the seal and wanting to witness the extraordinary moment when the whale leaps out of the water, grabs its prey and splashes back. What I would really want is for the whale to jump, grab the seal, shake it around, and then accidentally let go. Fat chance! But that is exactly what happened. And we got it on film.

Meanwhile back in Hampstead was I about to witness a similar scenario? The age-old drama of prey and predator. Admittedly, a rubber toad is hardly as endearing as a baby seal, nor are any of the potential predators of North London quite as magnificent as an enormous black-and-white cetacean! But what was the Hampstead equivalent? The following morning I had more of a clue. Not one but three of the ducklings had been fished out of the ponds and scattered around. Two of them bore teeth marks, the third had had the top of its head bitten clean off. One thing was emerging – whatever was doing this had developed a taste for synthetic materials. I assumed this was not its natural diet. The tooth damage suggested it was not a vegetarian. I feared the worst and I got it. Or something very close to it. My beloved Toady – my birthday present, my new best friend – was not in his official position. He was on the other side of the lawn, on his back. His legs were in the air, except for the one that was bitten in two, and he was completely headless. He was not, however, deflated, even if I was. Instead of being full of air, he was stuffed with some kind of white foam rubber. The sort of stuff people pack round delicate artefacts if they haven't got any dry mealworms. I had no doubt at all that the vandal – toad murderer and rubber fetishist – was a fox.

I hadn't seen a fox in the garden for quite some time. I missed them. Indeed, if I were honest, I would get much more excitement out of looking at a real live fox than at a rubber toad. So far however, Foxy seemed more intent on leaving bizarre clues to his crimes than on letting himself be seen. He was clearly well schooled in the conventions of TV crime series. Indeed he was to prove that in many ways he had quite a talent for entertaining an audience. Meanwhile, I was loathe to completely say goodbye to Toady. He was beyond revival or repair, and yet still quite imposing if I placed him with what used to be his head stuck down a gap in the rocks as if he were exploring what was down there. I wouldn't have called his warty rump and back legs his best angle, but it added a little humour to the scene. Well, it made me chuckle. Maybe Foxy found it quite amusing too. He certainly didn't molest or move it any further. Nevertheless, every morning it was a challenge to spot the result of whatever he had been up to the previous night.

Basically, it became obvious that Foxy liked moving things around and, let's face it, in my garden there was plenty to move around.

He seemed to have forsaken gratuitous vandalism. Instead of biting or gnawing my fake birds or animals, he simply repositioned them. I would come out and realise that my plastic Blackbirds were no longer grouped around a plant pot, but were now gathered in a corner of a flowerbed. I could almost hear Foxy muttering 'That looks better,' and then turning on my pretend rabbit warren and rearranging the bunnies in different sizes. A process which I imagine went right against the grain for a fox, to whom baby rabbits are generally regarded as food. Being a very intelligent fox, he presumably knew that none of my menagerie was edible. He'd made his mistake with that mouthful of rubber toad.

Actually, he very nearly made a much worse mistake that could've proved fatal to him. I went out into the garden one morning to hear the puzzling humming noise of what sounded like a muffled two-stroke engine. This is an often-quoted aide-memoire for the churring song of the Nightjar. Being the ancient birder that I am, I often quote the cliché that 'anything can turn up anywhere at any time.' Of course it isn't true. I simply refuse to believe that an albatross will ever fly over Hampstead Heath, or that I will ever hear a Nightjar singing in my garden. So what was this odd noise I was hearing? I traced the sound to the edge of my largest pond, in which I have fixed a medium-sized water fountain, powered by a submerged pump driven by electricity from a socket in my garden shed. The fountain wasn't much more than a trickle now, although the pump was still grinding away. However, it was no longer in the pond. It was at least a metre away, on the pebble shoreline. The scenario was surely indisputable. Foxy had decided he didn't like the positioning of the fountain, so he had tried to shift it. In doing so he discovered that:

a) the pump was heavy; and b) it was connected by a sturdy black flex, which was presumably waterproof. It was not however toothproof, and it was still live! What were the odds against him *not* biting through the wire and electrocuting himself? A Grey Squirrel had met just such an end in drier circumstances. I found it with its teeth still firmly clamped on the live flex that had powered the garden lights, but didn't again until I had removed the electrocuted squirrel, repaired the flex, and changed the fuse.

Foxy got away with it and learnt a lesson. He never again went near fountains or flex. Instead, he reverted to his garden ornament rearrangement routine. Somehow, it was too precise to be a random game. It was as if he was methodically positioning objects for beneficial, artistic or meaningful effect. We began to refer to him as Feng Shui Fox – there is surely an animated kids' TV series there? His main fetish seemed to be that he did not like items by the ponds, and so he moved them onto the cleaner canvas of the lawn. There he would arrange his patterns. Artists would call them 'installations.' A turtle next to a plastic hedgehog. A rubber snake alongside a Buddha. I whimsically began to conjecture that there might be some mystical meaning to his creations. I even discussed the idea with my psychotherapist, with whom I was at the relatively entertaining stage when depression had waned and I was given to flippancy, which may have been a trifle manic but was a lot more fun. I couldn't wait to regale my shrink with news of Foxy's latest activity, or was it a message? It was at least surely symbolic. To a therapist everything is. This time Foxy had utilised two objects. One was a toothily ferocious plastic crocodile. The other was a small plastic statue of Jesus Christ. Foxy had taken the reptile from beside my smallest pond and placed it in the very middle of the lawn.

He must then have crossed to the opposite side of the garden and removed the statue of Jesus from the discarded saucepan where he was apparently walking on water, although he had actually been resting on a piece of glass from a broken mirror. Presumably with all the gentleness and care with which I have seen foxes steal duck eggs, he had positioned our Lord with a raised hand bestowing a blessing on the crocodile. The alignment was neat beyond coincidence.

At my therapy session all talk of childhood deprivation was put aside as the doctor pondered the significance of Feng Shui Fox's latest offering. He was in doubt about its meaning: 'It is the classic juxtaposition. Good against Evil. Beastliness – the crocodile – against graciousness – Jesus.'

'Oh,' I commented. 'And who is the fox?'

He paused. 'He's just a fox.' I presumed we were both joking, but sometimes I still wonder.

I knew that Foxy wasn't joking when my wife was disturbed in the middle of the night by clattering and clonking on the patio just below her bedroom window. I was away working, which was a shame, as I would have loved to have seen what she did. There below her was Foxy, apparently conducting a meticulous search of the three or four crates we keep outside if the fridge is full. There was the residue of a recent party, with a box or two of canned lagers and a small selection of wines. Laura watched as Foxy worked his way along the crates, pulling out occasional cans or bottles as if checking the vintage. Even when Laura tapped on the window and shouted 'Oi,' he merely gave her a rather patronising glance, rejected a Pinot Grigio, knocked over an empty Prosecco bottle, and wandered off into the night with an air of one who wouldn't dream of touching alcohol anyway and regarded the fact that we obviously did as sinful. Either that, or he couldn't find a way of opening wine bottles and beer cans. Sad to relate that we did not see Feng Shui Fox again. Maybe his work was at an end. I'll tell you something though, if I ever see another giant rubber toad I shall purchase it immediately and place it right in the middle of the lawn with a 'welcome home' sign on it, and Foxy can move it wherever he likes.

Establishing a Preference

You may or may not recall that some pages ago I nonchalantly mentioned the relationship between Jesus Christ and a Great Tit. Sounds a bit like the introduction to a sermon – one of those tortuous analogies that radio vicars seem so found of. First there is a bit of banter with the disc jockey – often the late and lovely Terry Wogan – and then the guest spiritual guide blatantly switches to the script that he's been working on all weekend. Maybe he even tried it out on his congregation on Sunday. It starts something like: 'You know, there is nothing I enjoy more than feeding the birds in my garden. I just sit there quietly and the tits and Robins come to me to be fed and cared for. They are so dependent and so trusting. It strikes me that we humans are just like those tits. We trust Jesus to feed us. Okay he fed his followers loaves and fishes, whilst we put out peanuts and fat balls, but both are equally nourishing. They are both the food of love.'

I am not sure I would put it like that, but I won't argue with the love thing. I am sure all garden owners would agree that filling up the feeders is indeed an act of love. It is also an opportunity for studying the behaviour of the birds, much as Len Howard did years ago. Thus began my highly scientific observations which I entitled: 'Does it matter where it comes from?' It was inspired by the fact that no sooner have I appeared at the back door than several birds instantly appear, positively palpitating with expectation.

My Robins are definitely psychic. I swear they can sense my movements inside the house. I tested this by going into the back room and finding a Robin already waiting by the window. However, instead of going out with his mealworms I went back into the kitchen and then hurried upstairs to what we call the telly room, where a narrow glass door opens out onto a balcony. I walked towards it, only to find that the Robin had got there first. He was standing at the window already. I didn't feed him there either, but ducked out of sight and scuttled down into the back room again. There, waiting by the window was – you guessed it – the Robin. This time I went out to the garden to serve the mealworms and seeds. In one delicate dip the Robin took a beakful and flitted away, whilst giving me a glance that surely said: 'Thanks Bill. You know that you can run, but you can never hide.' A minute later I had both Blue Tits and Great Tits frantically grabbing food off my hand. By the way, both species nip. Blue Tit is barely a tickle, Great Tit is more like an injection.

As I sat at the garden table and watched the near feeding frenzy, my mind began mulling. First, I wondered if these birds would have been just as fearless if some other person was distributing the rations. Do they know a stranger when they see one? Although to be honest there aren't many strangers wandering through my garden. Smokers are banished out there, but they are usually also drinkers, so I don't suppose the birds find it a very tranquil atmosphere. At which point, my eyes began to wander round in search of a couple of non-human substitutes with which I could conduct an experiment. My idea was to use the fake humans as food dispensers and see if the birds had any preferences. I could of course have selected a couple of gnomes, but that seemed a bit of a cliché, besides which none of them looked remotely human. Unlike the two tiny but accurately moulded plastic figurines that were gathered round the sunken saucepan full of water. Do you remember that, and them? Most conspicuous, walking on the water – well, face down in it actually – was Jesus. An agreeable likeness, dressed in a flowing gown, and mercifully devoid of scars and wounds. It was presumably a pre-crucifixion image, with a cheery smile under his beard and, most appropriately, hinged arms that meant his hands could be adjusted, as if he were blessing, waving or offering food. For example, peanuts or mealworms. I even wondered if he was really meant to be St Francis of Assisi, but no, it was definitely the King of Kings.

Or was it? By extraordinary coincidence, or maybe it was a gesture of frivolous sacrilege (Foxy's last joke?), opposite Jesus on the rim of the saucepan there stands a statuette of the King of Rock and Roll, Elvis Presley. He is about the same size as Jesus and is indulging in some very un-Jesus like activity with a plastic mermaid. Being half tail, she can't stand up, but she is curled at exactly the right height to perform the relevant service. Nudge nudge. 'You can stop that,' I told both mermaid and Elvis,

'I have another task for you. And you Jesus. We are going to find out who really is 'the King' as far as the birds are concerned.'

Thus the scene was set. I cleared the garden of any other sources of food. I placed Jesus at one end of the garden table and Elvis at the other. I can't say that either of them were exactly designed for holding bird food, and of course I wanted the experiment to be completely fair and equal. I ended up with three or four peanuts on each figure. I could sense hyper-hungry tits chattering impatiently in the nearby bushes. The moment I withdrew, in they swooped.

And they continued to sweep in and out for the half hour or so that the experiment continued. I kept a meticulous count of what bird took what food from which king. Finally, I felt I had enough data to make valid conclusions.

The most obvious fact wasn't surprising, which was that Blue Tits are soppy and Great Tits are bullies. The second obvious fact was that none of the birds showed the slightest compunction about taking food from plastic figurines of famous figures, which slightly makes you wonder about the need to buy expensive feeders from the garden centre. But here comes the one you are waiting for. Did the birds show a preference? Which King did they take their food from? The answer was Elvis. By a mile. What's more, and remember that I am merely observing and recording the facts, especially the Great Tits seemed to actively dislike the Messiah. Far from avoiding him, they frequently knocked him flying. I suppose you might argue that this was a quicker way of getting at the food, but it didn't work because the peanuts just rolled off the table and started a free for all. To confirm my suspicions, I reunited Elvis with his mermaid by the saucepan, and I placed Jesus back upright alone on the table, but no sooner had I done so, than one or two Great Tits knocked him flying again. Meanwhile, Elvis stood tall and dispensed his nuts to everyone's delight, including his mermaid groupie. It was almost as if nature was mirroring life.

Oh Rats

Some years ago I was filming a sequence in the middle of a town through which ran a shallow river. It didn't look particularly clean and the banks were distressingly strewn with the usual detritus of cans, bottles, plastic bags and the occasional shopping trolley, although on closer inspection the water was pretty clear. We were able to film a sequence of my fingers rummaging around in the pebbles and eventually holding up my hand with a crayfish clinging to my thumb. What's more it was a native British White-clawed Crayfish, whose presence testified to the fact that this was chalk stream which, if we followed it into greener areas, would be an example of one of our most charming habitats (it is, of course, threatened). I wondered if there were Water Voles there. I recalled that the first one I ever saw was in an even more urban location in the north-east of England. We had filmed a small family of them scampering through a discarded trolley from the nearby supermarket.

At which point I dropped my crayfish as I glimpsed what looked like a diminutive tugboat crossing the river about 50 yards away. I knew what it was. So did the director and cameraman. We moved a little closer and set up the tripod. We had a short wait. Then I glimpsed a wake leading under an overhanging willow. Another short wait, then a nose, whiskers, feet and fur. I began a deceitful whispered commentary. 'There. Just peeping out. Little pink ears. Lovely twitchy whiskers. Beautiful brown fur. Look look, he's got something to nibble. Paws up to his mouth. Giving his ears a good wash. Isn't that cute? Do you know what it is? That's right. It's a rat!'

I wouldn't say that rats are my favourite creatures in the world, but they are pretty fascinating, and yes they are cute, especially the babies that have fur like grey velvet. Oh and just for the record, Water Voles do look rather lovely, even balancing on shopping trollies and especially if you are lucky enough to see one sitting there nibbling a reed-stem. Let me tell you, though, that if you are doing a Water Vole survey and you catch one in a humane trap and have to transfer it into a bag, you'd better wear armoured gloves because they can bite through steel and certainly through fingers.

So, back to ratty. Real ratty. Not the misidentified one that gets the wind in the willows, but the ratty – or ratties – that visit my garden. For a while I tried to pass them off as mice. Before that I simply didn't mention them to either my wife Laura or my daughter Rosie. To be honest neither of them were frequent visitors to the garden, but now and then they did go out there for a fag, or if the weather was really nice we might even indulge in an al fresco Sunday lunch. It was during one of those meals that Laura eventually spotted something small and furry scurrying around underneath the bird table. It was at the end of the garden, so it didn't justify a jumping on the table and screaming response, nor my impression of the cook in *Tom and Jerry*: 'Thomas! Where is that cat?' As it happens in my garden Thomas, or any other cat, would be less welcome than any number of rats (but more of that in a later chapter).

In fact it transpired that there were a number of rats scavenging in the garden, which meant that neither Laura nor Rosie would go out there until they had been disposed of. Frankly, I had little sympathy. If they decided to restrict themselves to staying inside the house that was their loss, as long as they didn't smoke in there. I am as intolerant about smoking as Laura is about rats in the garden, even if they were very small rats with great big ears and sweet little faces. Their only really rat-like feature was their long and rather unnaturally rubbery tails. I even managed to convince Laura that they weren't utterly repulsive, and to be fair, she conceded as much. However, I knew that it was only a matter of quite a short time before she made the announcement that I knew was imminent, and was dreading: 'We are going to have to get a man in.' To me that means poison, the slaughter of wildlife and, worst of all, an affront to my ingenuity and possibly my masculinity.

We not infrequently have mice in the house, and whilst they can certainly make even me jump when one zips across in front of the telly and disappears up the curtains, I have caught enough of them in humane traps and carried them out to freedom on Hampstead Heath for Laura to accept that the situation is under control. There has been a certain amount of discussion about how far you have to take them away from the house to be sure that they won't find their way back in... well, there has been discussion about that too. It is a topic worth bringing up when the dinner party is flagging. Opinions are very variable. Some folk say a hundred metres, others say two or three miles, and that if you release them in the evening they'll be back by dawn. I daresay there are tales of 'homing mice' that were released in America and swam back across the Atlantic.

My mouse-releases tend to be influenced by the weather. If it is bucketing down I have been known to apologetically drop a mouse into next door's garden and fib to Laura, whilst on a clement evening it might be given the expansive freedom of Parliament Hill. I entirely approve of humane mousetraps. Not only is the success rate pretty high (chocolate bait works well), but you get a delightful close up of the little fella before letting him or her go.

'We have never had a man in to deal with the mice,' I announce to Laura, 'and we shall never have a man in for the rats. Correction, we already have a man in. Me.'

I think I may have dissembled a little when I promised Laura that I would be putting down rat-sized versions of the humane mousetraps. Secretly, I had to admit to myself that I wasn't entirely confident about handling a rat myself. This despite the fact that I had handled the majority of British rodents, and indeed been bitten by most of them. Moreover, I knew at least two friends – both female as it happens – who owned, loved, and cuddled pet rats. Mind you pet rats are always white, as if that denotes that they are friendly. Wild rats are not friendly.

Nevertheless, I certainly wished them no harm. I set myself to do a little research on how to rid your house or garden of rats without harming them. I was delighted and frankly surprised to discover at least three articles that explained that rats are easily deterred by encountering unfamiliar objects placed close to their nests. The article didn't go on to explain the psychology. Did the rats freak out at the disturbance, or was it an aesthetic objection? 'Oh no, who put that in front of our hole?' Neither were there any suggestions about what kind of objects were most effective. However, I felt honour-bound, and more than a little curious, to give it a go.

I didn't know exactly where the rat's nest was, but I was guessing that it was somewhere murky under the shed. Close by was a lilac tree with two sloping trunks rooted close to a wooden bird table. It was of course the spilled birdseed under the table that attracted ground-feeders like Dunnocks and pigeons, and several very young rats. Their approach was always the same. Presumably they left their nest, then shinned up a lilac trunk until they reached another branch which sloped down to the ground, just beside the spilled seed area. Bird table above, rat table below, as it were. They were delightful little animals and obviously committed to their routine, as at the slightest disturbance – a passing Sparrowhawk, for example – they would scamper back up using exactly the same route they had come down.

Even though what I was about to do was utterly harmless, I still felt sad about discouraging them. Hopefully it wouldn't be too traumatic. Hopefully also it would work. I began modestly, by placing a coloured ball exactly where they made their first appearance. Two rats sort of sniffed it, went round it, and carried on nibbling. I gave that a day or two thinking maybe they needed to get used to it. Then it struck me that they were meant *not* to get used to it. I removed the ball and replaced it with a medium-sized gnome. One rat went round it. Another climbed up and sat on the gnome's knee. The following days, I tried a few of my plastic birds, including a falcon, a parrot and a duck. No reaction, except I realised that there were at least four baby rats. I also realised that they were getting bigger, but were still cute.

My next move was to not replace or remove any objects but instead to let them accumulate. I imagined the kids toddling down the lilac branch in the morning to be greeted by the ever-growing parade under the bird table. Were they aware of new additions – 'Hey, there's a stone hedgehog' – or did they notice positional changes? – 'Wasn't there a gnome there?'

I was about to surrender and put all the unfamiliar objects – which by now were quite familiar – back in their places, when I had what I thought had to be the ultimate deterrent. The décor of the first-floor landing in our Disney-esque house had a nautical theme. There were driftwood mirrors, wooden fishes, frames full of nautical knots, and a rather fine statue of Lord Nelson. There was also a ship's cat. Not of course a real cat – can you imagine me having one of those? I bought this one from a nautical knick-knack shop in Covent Garden. It was sort of ginger-coloured, a bit scruffy and – here's the thing – extremely realistic. I'll be honest, I would have assumed it had been stuffed if the lady in the shop hadn't told me otherwise. 'You mean someone made it? From what?' I decided not to go there, but the cat came with me.

Rather gleefully, I placed the totally realistic cat on the floor at the foot of the lilac tree. It wasn't floppy, it was fixed in a sort of lounging posture, but with its teeth slightly bared and its eyes squinting ominously.

If I were a Blue Tit I would've flown a mile. Or a Great Tit, or a Robin. But they didn't. I peeped out next morning to see most of the usual birds hopping around behind and on top of the realistic cat, and – to bring the experiment to a close – one, two, three, all four little rats were playfully chasing around the cat, until one popped up on its shoulder, bent down, and – I could swear – gave it a kiss.

I have to confess I cannot remember how this episode ended. I may have lied to Laura when she asked: 'Have you got rid of those rats?'

'No need,' I may have replied, 'They just went. I'd forgotten they were ever there.'

Or maybe I agreed that she could get a man in – not every husband is so tolerant. Or maybe she waited until I was away for a week or two. All I do know is that for quite some time I saw very few rats in the garden, but it wasn't the 'unfamiliar object' routine that was keeping them away. Or maybe it was. After all, the unfamiliar objects continue to proliferate so maybe the rats just can't stand it anymore. Oh no, wait a minute, there was one extraordinary exception.

A Job for the Pied Piper

The year 2015 was our *annus horribilis*, though it pains me even to distinguish it with anything so sophisticated as Latin. We live in a Victorian-type terrace with the houses in pairs – technically 'semis,' but not as we usually think of them. For many years our next-door neighbours had been amiable and above all quiet. Even though they had had to tolerate our parties and band practices, which must have been audible next door if not in the next street, not once had we had cause to complain of disturbance except on the occasion when the man of the house sat on his balcony shooting at pigeons. In that instance somebody called the police when they heard gunfire. Fire enough. After that the only sound was the 'tiddly-tum, tiddly-tum, woo-woo' of his toy train whose track circled his garden, or rather the swimming pool which was his garden. It is surely indicative of a peaceful person that they could have a swimming pool and yet manage to avoid teenage parties with splashing, screaming and very loud music. We thank those neighbours.

Alas, early in 2015 we got the news that the quiet folks next door were 'downsizing' and had sold their house to an American family. We never met the new owners. Before they could move in they intended (threatened?) to give the house a makeover. This is a euphemism for completely gutting it and totally transforming it. Filling in the garden (the pool), smashing out walls, reshaping rooms, and so forth. The constant cacophony was achieved by a battalion of nightmare noisemakers, including pneumatic drills, steam hammers, saws and sanders, and a team of builders with voices so loud they could drown out Status Quo in concert. When work was finally completed the Americans announced that they weren't moving in at all, and they sold the house for five million pounds. Well, well – what a surprise. Fortunately for us the new owners, as well as presumably being extremely well off, are incredibly gentle and quiet. Phew. So what's this got to do with rats?

At first I wasn't aware of any connection. Then one morning I spotted an adult rat snuffling around in a flowerbed. It was joined by another, and then a third. This was not usual. A pair was as many as we'd had before, except for the little family under the lilac tree (which incidentally, now bears a placard commemorating 'The Rat Run'). The following day there were five of them lined up almost in orderly fashion along a rotting log. It was about then that Laura spotted them. Inevitably there was talk about a man being got in. I could of course offer no gentler alternative, but I pleaded with her to give it a few more days. I suggested that maybe these rats were just passing through. 'Well I hope there aren't any more,' she reasonably requested.

Her request was ignored. And how. I have never witnessed anything like it. I was about to open the back door to go and feed the garden birds when I realised that they weren't the only ones on the feeders. Well I say on. Also under and in. At the risk of echoing the Pied Piper, there were rats hanging on the peanuts, there were rats on the suet block, rats on the sunflower seeds, and rats on what was left of the mealworms. Neither were they simply hanging and nibbling, they were literally cascading over the fence like a miniature reconstruction of wildebeest migration. There were all ages, all sizes. Many of them climbed up the trunk of the chestnut by the window, from where they literally threw themselves at dangling feeders. At one point one of the cage-type feeders was crammed with one rat after another, until there were so many in there that they couldn't get out. When I finally opened the back door, the ones in the cage panicked, and bit and scratched each other to escape. Having done so, they simply let themselves fall to the floor and joined in another feeding frenzy. At one point I estimated there were at least 100 of them. It looked like panic. It looked like escape. Was it migration, or was it eviction? I admit it was more than a little scary.

Amazingly, by the next day there were only a few of them left, and a few days after that they seemed to have gone. Nevertheless, this was the one occasion I had to agree that Laura's solution was justified. We got a man in. He placed a few not-so-humane traps in dark places around the edges of the garden. Naturally, I described what we had seen. His explanation was that: 'Rats are very sensitive to noise.'

To which I responded that they ought to have moved out months ago when the Americans had started their makeover. He then asked if there had been any recent drilling downwards, for pipe or sewer work. There most certainly had been. All last week. 'Rats can sense the vibrations,' he said.

'So could we,' I retorted. I anticipated the explanation and continued.

'So if they were rats in the olden days living underground and they felt vibrations, they'd know that meant there was an earthquake on the way, or a volcano about to erupt, and they would flee for their lives.'

Exactly. 'Let's get out of here. Over the fence. Into Bill Oddie's garden. We'll be safe there.'

'But what if they get a man in?'

'Just don't go in the little green boxes.'

You know, I can still envisage that day. I can't help wondering whether all those hundred and odd rats were living next door? And if so, where are they now?

Parakeets and Dentists' Drills

The Ring-necked Parakeet – sometimes known by the prettier name of Rose-ringed Parakeet – is native to South Asia, particularly India, and parts of Africa. In Britain they were never seen outside a cage or aviary until the early 1960s, when a small number appeared to be flying and breeding free in south London. It is possible that some careless bird fancier simply left the cage open. There is an appealing but probably totally fictitious urban myth that Jimi Hendrix's girlfriend kept a few parakeets as pets until one evening, when freedom and probably dope was in the air, Jimi himself flung open a window and bade the birds take flight to the strains of the plangent chords of *Wild Thing*, his version being so much more majestic than that of The Troggs.

Personally I have no wish to deflate that theory, but I do have to concede that a more plausible scenario is that a local movie studio (there are still several in that area) was filming a new version of

The African Queen and shipped in a consignment of parakeets. This was a mistake in more than one way. Firstly, Ring-necked Parakeets are most numerous in India, not Africa. And secondly, one suspects that when the film had wrapped (technical movie talk for finished), instead of gifting the birds to a local zoo, they simply let them go. In my experience wrap parties soon descend into raucous and irresponsible behaviour, and I can easily imagine the climax of the evening involving parakeet racing, or testing if they would return like homing pigeons. Subsequent events indicate that most of them didn't. Instead they divided into pairs and sought out suitable nest holes in local parks and gardens. By the time I filmed them for my TV birding series there was a spectacular gathering every night in the grounds of Esher Rugby Club. I remember it vividly, not least because I started the sequence by attempting to kick a rugby ball between the posts – something I last did when I was about 20 years of age. Much to the amusement of five thousand parakeets, I imagine, I ruptured a calf muscle and a hamstring, and my whole leg turned dark blue and remained that way for a month.

Sometimes 'escaped' populations eventually fade away and disappear, but not these parakeets. Nowadays their stronghold is still south-west London, but they are established just about everywhere around the capital and there are frequent reports of them moving into other parts of the country. They have in fact now been accepted as an 'official' British bird. Call them aliens, call them immigrants if you like, but Ring-necked Parakeets are no longer foreigners. I was extolling this fact not many years ago in Richmond Park, and allaying all accusations that they were competing with and displacing native species that share similar habitat.

As if to prove it, we filmed an enormous gnarled tree that had enough holes and crevices to accommodate not only parakeets but also Jackdaws, Nuthatches and a pair of Great Spotted Woodpeckers. They each had a hole as a home, close to one another, but with no apparent squabbling. There would be the occasional tiff over a beakful of buds, but almost invariably the newcomers gave way to the more established species. Parakeets have hooked beaks, but they use them to pluck food, to snap at a rival male, or to nuzzle a mate. Moreover, surely no one would deny that they are real good-lookers. Red beak, rose neck-rings, lemon yellow in the tail-streamers, and otherwise green green green.

I concluded my piece to camera by officially welcoming Ring-necked Parakeets to our country, confident that they would be embraced by all. But I was wrong. As I was leaving Richmond Park a stately lady of intermediate age and undeniable good breeding accosted me rather belligerently.

'Mr Oddie. Were you filming the parakeets?' It wasn't so much a question as an accusation. Then came the question: 'How are you going to get rid of them?'

I responded with a couple of questions of my own: 'Why should we get rid of them?' and 'Why me?'

She conceded that the control of unpopular British birds is not my job and transferred the responsibility for a parakeet cull to the government. In the past I have been personally blamed for allowing the proliferation of magpies, 'seagulls,' cormorants and crows.

I suppressed my instinct to mention badgers, but instead asked her the leading question: 'Why do you want to get rid of parakeets?'

I admit I was quite surprised by her answer: 'Because they don't belong here.'

I couldn't believe she believed it herself. 'Not because they might displace native species then?'

'Do they? Well I wouldn't know about that.'

'Well they don't actually. So is it because they are noisy?'

'No. No. I don't mind that.'

I was genuinely puzzled. 'So what do you mind?'

'I mind that they are here and they shouldn't be. Because they are not British.' With that she called her poodle and flounced off towards Southall, which ironically is one of the most multiracial areas in London.

I couldn't resist a parting shot. 'That sounds like racism to me madam. And that dog doesn't look very British.'

To be honest I have never encountered anything quite like that level of bias until Brexit. However, what I, and most people in London and beyond, have encountered is plenty of Ring-necked Parakeets. They have undoubtedly become an established garden bird around the capital. It is undeniable that they do have some habits which do not endear them to everybody. As it happens, what we feared could be their greatest sin is yet to be proved. There is very little evidence that they are driving out native hole-nesting species, which may simply indicate that – especially in London parks – there is no shortage of holes in trees. Also, from my observations they appear to be a bit wimpish. They don't mind a good squabble – usually hanging off a branch or a feeder – but it is usually with one of their own kind. Show them a couple of Great Tits hanging on the peanuts and they will wait their turn. However, there is no question that they will gobble up seeds and nuts that aren't theoretically meant for them. Mind you, let's face it, Feral Pigeons are even worse. The answer to deterring any greedy interlopers is to use feeders with a cage around them, or with very small seed portals. It won't stop them trying, but most times they lose their balance or fall off, which will provide you with hours of fun.

So m'lud, I contest that, to all intents and purposes, Ring-necked Parakeets are not harmful. However, I do admit that they are very noisy.

Several thousand at the Esher roost was cacophonous and I have to concede that a small flock of half a dozen zipping low out of my garden isn't what you'd call mellifluous. Personally, I positively like it since I have heard much the same raucous chorus in rainforests all over the world from Panama to Papua New Guinea. However, I have to accept that not everyone is so enamoured with the squawky squadrons. For example, my neighbours. Firstly, let me make a couple of things clear. The folks next door are extremely amiable and friendly and – so important in neighbours – we all keep an eye on whatever is going on in the street, be it house and car alarms going off, drunken teenagers, burst pipes, that sort of thing. Secondly, they are not called Derek and Lynn, but I see no reason to use their real names.

One morning a couple of years ago I discovered that whilst I was delighted that garden visits from parakeets were becoming more frequent, and I found their version of the dawn chorus was a perfectly cheery way to start the day, Derek and Lynn did not agree. One day I was emerging from my front door just as Derek opened his. At the same moment the green arrows screamed from the direction of my garden, swooped back even more noisily, and gathered at the top of an adjacent fir tree, chattering to one another.

I smiled at Derek. He did not reciprocate. I half-expected the famous 'When are you going to get rid of them?' request, but Derek knew better since he had heard me moan about the public's response to wild things before. Instead, his voice almost pleaded for sympathy. 'Bill, surely you can't like that noise, can you?'

I was honest. 'Well… I don't exactly like it, but I don't dislike it. I don't really notice it.'

'But it is unbearable' he winced. 'They wake us up before dawn. And sometimes we can't get to sleep.'

'Oh come on,' I protested, 'They aren't nocturnal.'

'Lynn likes an afternoon nap.'

At which point Lynn herself came up with a metaphor she had presumably been working on: 'That screeching goes right through you… It's like a dentist's drill.'

'Exactly darling,' agreed Derek, 'A dentist's drill. That's what they are like. A dentist's drill.'

I don't mind disagreement, but I won't tolerate inaccuracy. It instantly aroused the pedant in me. I said, 'Lynn, I can accept that some people – for example yourself, or you, Derek – don't like that noise, and you may well liken it to various other objectionable noises, but Ring-necked Parakeets do not in anyway whatsoever sound like a dentist's drill.'

'Insofar as it is a nasty noise, it does,' muttered Derek defiantly.

'Exactly,' Lynn agreed, 'I didn't mean that they sounded exactly the same as a dentist's drill. I just meant they make a very nasty noise.'

'What?' I replied, 'You mean like the ambulance sirens that pass by every five minutes, or the BMW driver that stops at the lights every morning with his window open playing thump thump thump music, or that bloody leaf blower and hedge trimmer, or the helicopter that hovers overhead at least twice every day and none of us know why. Personally I find all those noises far more grating than a small flock of dazzling little birds.'

As Derek and Lynn got into their car I fired a parting shot: 'You wanna try living in Australia mate. Not just parakeets. Parrots, cockatoos, lorikeets, rosellas, galahs, budgies, kookaburras.'

'They're not parakeets,' retorted Lynn.

'No, but they make a hell of row.'

I had a feeling this one was going to run and run. As they drove off I heard Derek's defiant resolve: 'There must be something we can do to scare them away.'

There was! A week or two later I was in my garden when I saw something unfamiliar next door. It looked like a fishing rod held vertically, but it began growing upwards, higher and higher, longer and longer. The fence between our gardens is as high as the council will allow, so I was able to estimate that this rod was at least 10 feet long, maybe longer. Certainly high enough to snag in an overhanging tree, at which point whoever was holding it must have lost their balance and it toppled out of sight. I presumed it was Derek's initial attempt at a parakeet deterrent, but I thought it less troublesome if I kept quiet. After quite a long pause, the rod again began to rise, but this time it looked even more like a fishing rod since it had a metre of line with a hook on the end. There was obviously something dangling from the hook. It began to reveal itself. Two huge red-rimmed eyes rose into sight over the fence. They were attached to a black-and-yellow triangular body and a diamond string of a tail. It was clearly a paper kite. I presumed it was Chinese and was meant to be a stylised image either of a googly-eyed bird or a dragon. It may have been designed to be flown in ceremonial parades in Chinatown, from whence I assumed it had come. Or perhaps this what you find if you Google 'bird scarer.' I doubt that it was specific to parrots, but for Derek it was worth a go, and anyway I couldn't stop him. In any case, I didn't want to.

For the first week I merely observed. It was particularly entertaining on windy days, when the bird scarer would swoop all over the place, now and again getting stuck in a big tree or snagged by the roses. Eventually it was blown across so that it dangled over my garden shed, at which point I protested that Derek was invading my airspace. He was not without humour, and I felt it only fair to warn him that such contraptions just don't work. Birds might be slightly puzzled by the initial encounter, but they soon suss out that a huge sheet of coloured paper is exactly that, and therefore constitutes no danger. I rather suspect that not long after that, Derek accepted that he wasn't going to chase off the parakeets but he grew rather fond of the Chinese bird kite, purely as a piece of outdoor decoration. Considering the bizarre baubles dangling in my garden, I could only approve. I even felt sympathy when he bought a second rod and another coloured kite, but the wind whisked it way up to the very top of an oak tree, where it dangles to this very day.

Meanwhile, in case you doubted it, the parakeets continued to perfect their dentist-drill impression. If anything their numbers increased.

Derek decided to have one last attempt. This time he went for realism. Well sort of. Once more my airspace was invaded, by what looked at first glance like a raggedy bird of prey.

I went out into the garden and called cheerily to Derek. 'It won't work you know.' It could be said that one of Derek's slight deficiencies is that he doesn't really listen. I decided to plough straight on. 'Look, Derek, do you see that plastic bird of prey on my shed roof? That is a Peregrine Falcon. It is very realistic. So is that one over there. That's a Gyr Falcon – a sort of Arctic Peregrine. And there are several owls. All very lifelike. And yet none of the birds that come into my garden take any notice of them. Birds are my job. I spend a lot of time taking photos in my garden. If what you have been trying to do – scaring birds away – really was working, I would be pretty annoyed. It's okay though, because I know it won't work. The Chinese kite didn't work and this new one *really* won't work. It's a bird of prey. Its meant to be a Red Kite, but Red Kites don't hunt small birds, they are scavengers, and in any case I don't think any birds will take a lot of notice of it when its hanging upside-down. Which it was.

The parakeets are thriving. So is Derek and Lynn's garden. In fact it has been given a professional, and I daresay pretty expensive, makeover. It is a bit formal for my taste, with rectangular flowerbeds, large areas of paving and lots of climbers on trellis, which I benefit from because some of them climb over the fence and flower on my side. I can imagine that Derek may feel it is unfair that his passionflower seems to prefer crawling all over my shed roof to sticking to his trellis where it belongs. Maybe they were a gift from the friendly gardener who also helped me to extend my bamboo thicket and had planted plenty of insect-enticing flowers. One thing that seems to be almost missing, however, is trees. There used to be a lovely big willow right in the middle of the lawn, but it has gone. Completely. The result is that Derek and Lynn rarely get parakeets in their garden as there's nowhere for them to perch.

.

Cat-astrophe

In contrast to Derek and Lynn's garden, mine has such a diverse array of trees that the parakeets can choose to perch on a different one every day. They can dangle from the willow, clamber around in the Silver Birch, shuffle up and down amongst the cotoneaster berries, and play hide-and-seek in the Horse Chestnut, as well as sliding up and down the wire holding up the peanut feeders, and even trying to poke the tips of their beaks through the wire mesh which protects the tray of live food. To be honest I have yet to see a parakeet eat a mealworm, dead or alive, but then it is my theory that it is not the food itself that delights the parakeets, it is the acrobatic challenges that they enjoy. In fact, I think of parakeets as the avian equivalent to gibbons. They both just love swinging around. Moreover they both have very loud voices, although when it comes to singing the gibbons definitely have the best tunes.

Not that I have gibbons in my garden, but I know someone who does and they don't live in the tropics either. I once visited a lady who runs a gibbon rescue centre in South Carolina, USA. She lives on a charming suburban housing estate. The residents no doubt value its calm, quiet and tranquillity. They must have been somewhat perturbed when they heard that their imminent new neighbours were to be at a couple of dozen gibbons. They had witnessed the construction of enclosures, cages, free-range areas and overnight accommodation, all surrounded by a reassuringly strong, sturdy and high gibbon-proof fence. There was even a small neighbourhood welcoming posse to greet the arrival of the new tenants, who for the moment appeared docile and shy and clung to the lady and her fellow keepers, burying their heads bashfully and craving comfort and affection. The neighbours were enchanted. They no doubt went to bed with smiles on their faces.

Until the next morning when, just before dawn, the gibbons awoke and did what all gibbons do — they sang. First a solo, then a duet, then more and more, louder and louder, until it became a chorus or a cacophony. Your reaction to such a noise probably differs depending on whether you are standing in the magic natural echo-chamber of the rainforest, or trying to have a peaceful snooze in a sedate neighbourhood in South Carolina. The neighbours were no doubt alarmed, but wished to be accommodating — after all, there is some kudos in telling people you live in an estate full of gibbons. But they needed their sleep. Fortunately, my friend, the gibbon mother, solved the problem by imposing a strict schedule on the animals. There was to be no singing before nine in the morning. A rule the gibbons obeyed, because they weren't allowed outside until nine, or ten on Sundays. During the day they had to observe a couple of quiet hours, and the evening chorus, which is nearly as boisterous as the dawn chorus, must conclude no later than seven-thirty, or sometimes earlier if there was a big ball game on TV. Imagine trying to concentrate on the cup final with a bunch of gibbons whooping away. It'd be worse than those vuvuzela things that ruined the 2010 World Cup.

Enough of gibbons, although in my opinion it is not possible to ever have enough of gibbons. Be honest, I have a lot to thank them for, what with 'Funky Gibbon' reaching number two in the charts in 1976. But I am not trying to bask in past glories – or do I mean embarrassments? It is just that I like to think my Carolina gibbons story is rather a good example of how animals and humans can happily co-exist. Indeed they need to.

With one notable exception. Cats and me, and probably vice versa. People frequently confront me with not so much a question as an accusation. 'I suppose you don't like cats because they eat birds?'

'No,' I reply, 'It's not just that.' There are several reasons I don't much care for cats. For a start I find them a bit boring. They all look more or less the same. Okay, they come in a variety of coats, from fluffy ones that look like feather dusters to those creepy ones with no fur at all. Whatever the texture, they are all basically cat-shaped, but they are small versions of 'proper' wild cats like tigers, panthers, leopards, lynxes and so on, all of which to me are more handsome and impressive than the domestic version. Unsurprisingly, the only domestic cat that I find slightly attractive is a basic 'tabby,' simply because it most closely resembles a genuine Scottish Wildcat, especially as they have been known to confuse matters by interbreeding. I can't imagine, though, that the aloof, self-centred, dozy nature of most pet cats has been inherited from their wild ancestors, although their penchant for sneaking around killing garden birds probably is.

Dogs on the other hand are a simply wonderful illustration of the ancient adage that 'variety is the spice of life.' Dogs come in so many diverse shapes and sizes that it is hard to believe that they all belong to the same species. St Bernard, Chihuahua, Poodle – all dogs. They also vary in temperament, though surely few of us would deny that it is basically in the nature of most dogs to be friendly, faithful and anxious to please. These endearing qualities are clearly not inherited from their wild ancestors. Neither wolves nor dingos have placid reputations, and actual Wild Dogs are not only ferocious, they are disconcertingly ugly once past the puppy stage.

Let's face it, it is a huge tribute to human ingenuity that in domesticating dogs they have engineered a fantastic selection, custom-built for all sorts of tasks, from hunting and herding sheep to dancing on *Britain's Got Talent*, not to mention guiding the blind, sniffing out drugs and, most welcome of all, being invariably pleased to see you and – even more endearingly – not being afraid to show physical affection. It is almost as if a dog considers its main reason for existence is to make you feel wanted.

From my observations I have concluded that cats are interested only in being fed and perhaps getting a stroke or a tickle, neither of which are they able to properly reciprocate. Put it this way, I think that humanity would be more generous and agreeable if it were based on dogs, but more selfish and mean-spirited if it copied cats, to coin a phrase.

I assure you that I do not speak from total prejudice or lack of personal experience. There have been cats in my life, and even quite a few in my house. There was that white one that scared me when I was a little boy in Rochdale. Twenty-five years later my first wife Jean was accompanied by two cats. Muffler had, I admit, rather a sweet name, but with a slightly dark edge in that it implies the cosiness of cat fur for warm winter garments, which of course I wouldn't condone any more than I approve of fox-fur or seal-skin. Jean's second cat was called Cleese, named entirely so that I could have the satisfaction of saying 'I am taking Cleese down to the vet to get him neutered.'

During my first marriage I never risked a critical comment on either of the cats, partially because we also had dogs that didn't do much to make of a case for their own superiority. One of them continually escaped to Hampstead Heath and made it obvious that he would rather live with the receptionist at a hospital a mile or two away. So we let him. Then there was Daisy Dog, a typical Jack Russell whose only motivation for going walkies was to nibble old ladies' ankles. She was deported to the countryside where ladies wear higher wellies. Had I expressed the notion of getting rid of the cats I would've roused the ire of Jean and our two daughters. Frankly they were more likely to have got rid of me.

Ironically, in a sense that is what eventually happened. Our late 1970s almost-commune mainly worked pretty well, but as the decade wore on it became clear that its days were numbered. To cut a long and quite convoluted story short, eventually I met my wife to be, Laura. We 'got it on,' as we still said in those days, and began discussing cohabiting arrangements. There was only one problem. Or rather, would you believe, three problems. I am sure she genuinely sympathised.

She knew I wasn't a cat-lover, and if there had only been one I would surely have accepted that most girls in their mid-twenties came with a cat. But three? It pains me to have to admit it but I really did issue the classic ultimatum: 'I am sorry, but either they go or I do.' Probably not a day of our 30 years of marriage has gone by when she hasn't regretted ditching the moggies and sticking with me. At least I have lasted longer than they would have done.

Ever since then our house has remained a cat-free zone. And most of the time so has the garden, until relatively recently. I suppose I could regard it as an ironic tribute to how many garden birds are attracted to the feeders I put out. It is the old old story. Birds eat seed. Cats eat birds. If they can catch them.

'All cats kill birds. Except yours, you say?'

'My cat could never catch a bird. It's too fat.'

'Why? Do you feed it too much?'

'Of course not.'

'So why is it so fat? I'll tell you why. Because it's been eating garden birds.' All cats do, and will continue to until they make Blue Tit-flavoured cat food.'

I can imagine the label: 'Contains real Blue Tits, with just a hint of Robin. Caught in the traditional way in mist nets approved by the BTO.'

I am sorry, but I really don't accept this 'my cat is innocent' argument. All cats chase, catch, chew and bring the victim – dead or alive – in through the cat-flap, and leaving its remains on the kitchen floor. It is not part of the natural food chain, it is part of the gratuitously cruel chain, and it is a worldwide problem.

In my garden I was delighted to see that neighbours on both sides were doing garden makeovers, including brand new fences which were surely too tall and too smooth for a cat to climb. How wrong I was. A subsequent feline invader soon convinced me that a cat could scale the Eiger without crampons on its paws. Actually a cat does have crampons. They are called claws and they are very sharp, as anyone would attest who has had a friend's pet leap onto their lap and knead their thighs, a sentiment which in some circumstances could be construed as mildly erotic but in practice is bloody painful. Neither does it help if your friend says 'Oh he likes you. Funny, he always goes for people who don't like cats.' I personally don't agree. It is *not* funny. It is extremely painful.

Moreover, I concede that a cat's claws allow it to scale vertical surfaces, such as my garden fence. They can also squeeze through tiny gaps, tightrope walk along the top of fences, shin up tree trunks, and leap from a great height. All of which are demonstrated by new my arch-enemy, the neighbourhood psychocat. It is large, with black-and-white fur in a pattern that would be better suited to a Friesian cow. I suspect that the first time I saw it may have been its first visit to my garden, as it was rambling around as if it was a bit lost. More likely, in fact, that it was exploring and checking out the best places it could hide, so that it could get close to the birds on the feeders without them realising they were being stalked. Let's face it, a bird table must be like a fast food restaurant for a cat. Albeit for the moment the table was empty, as my garden birds had sensibly flown to the very top of the tallest tree, or maybe even retreated to nearby Hampstead Heath. They would come back eventually. Cats have patience. It intended to wait, but I didn't. I hurled myself out the back door. The cat shot away around the corner. I followed, but he had already completely disappeared. 'Mmm,' I told myself with a determined sigh, 'Let battle commence.'

Sometimes my family tease me by reporting Psycho's presence before I have seen him, and they pretend to like him. 'Oh isn't he handsome.' Or 'Aw look, he's having a catnap.'

I correct them. 'That cat is not napping, it is lurking. It is not snoozing, sun bathing or meditating. It is lurking with intent, and the intent is to wait until a garden bird hops near enough for it to be able to leap out from its lurking place and zap it with its paw, or paws, or jaws.'

The piebald predator mainly lurks under a small dense bush guarded by a gnome and a family of plastic Meerkats, or it crouches menacingly by a low raised flowerbed just outside the French windows (the only exit to the garden). Both these hiding places are within pouncing distance of small clusters of bird feeders, which are mainly advertised as 'squirrel-proof,' which is much the same thing as cat-proof. I have yet to see my pied villain leap and snatch a bird dangling from a feeder, however, there is inevitably a certain amount of seed spillage below the feeders which attracts the inveterate ground-feeders like Dunnocks and pigeons and the temporary scavengers such as Blue Tits, Great Tits, Robins, thrushes, and so on – birds which will eat just about anything from anywhere, heads down and oblivious that they could easily become a moggy meal.

The facts are uncomfortably incontrovertible. Cats are inveterate hunters and they kill millions of garden birds all over the world. I wish them no harm, but neither do I offer them a welcome. Especially my black-and-white nemesis. I had assumed that it came from next door, but I recently discovered that it belongs about 100 metres down the road in a house with a low front garden wall on which it poses like an ancient Egyptian deity. If it isn't posing it is presumably sleeping indoors, or lurking in my or someone else's garden.

Obviously I can't deny my neighbours' right to own a cat, even if I told them that I had reason to believe it is on a mission to obliterate every bird in Hampstead and in my garden in particular. I suspect their response would be: 'That's your problem, mate.' Indeed, and for literally months I have attempted to solve it.

For several weeks I practised an elaborate 'shoo' method, which involved leaping out of the French windows and doing my impression of a belligerent tomcat. This involved hissing and screeching, and even flapping my arms and clapping my hands, neither of which are typical tomcat behaviour. Whether the intruder thought I was a rival or a nutter I neither know nor care, because it was enough to startle him into scarpering over the fence propelled by my request: 'And don't come back.' But of course he soon did, and of course I cannot conduct the normal business of life if my schedule is constantly disrupted by obsessively racing round the garden doing cat impressions.

We all know that cats don't like water, but short of creeping up behind a cat that's hunched over the edge of a fishpond trying to skewer frogs and pushing it in, you have to arm yourself with some kind of water propellant. I soon concluded that a watering can was not designed for the job, One of those little plastic bottles for sprinkling seedlings or dampening the ironing are okay, but they don't have much range. I had no choice but to resort to the garden hosepipe. An accurately directed spray is effective, but just short of satisfying. What you would really relish is a powerful fire engine-type cascade that sends Mr Cat surfing away backwards over the garden fence as if on a reversed flume. Tom and Jerry, where are you when I need you? I accept that some of this might offend the animal welfare people, but I am one of them and I don't mind. I find that any insidious feelings of guilt are easily overcome by reminding myself that it is only water, and that even cats could do with a good wash now and then. Don't tell me all that pink-tongued licking business does the job.

So, water deterrents do work, but they rely on the cat having a decent memory. 'Well, I won't be going back to that garden again.'

'Good.'

'Even if that Song Thrush did look rather tasty.'

The other problem is (a lack of) rapid response. When you spot the cat, how quickly can you get out of the house, turn on the outside tap, unreel enough hosepipe, adjust the spray power on the nozzle and find the cat again. Which of course by then is back down the road posing on the wall and being stroked by passing cat-loving neighbours. It's probably even purring and doing that creepy arched-neck thing that cats do when they are pretending to love you.

Thus, as with everything these days, I have resorted to modern technology. I have purchased a various sonic and ultrasonic beams, which of course no cat on earth can tolerate. Except the ones that don't seem to mind them at all. Are they deaf, immune or blasé? In fact, my pied villain seems to actually enjoy these devices. I have two sonic weapons. One is a funnel-shaped plastic hand-gun that looks like a small loud hailer. It's called a 'Cat-a-pult,' which made me chuckle and mutter 'if only.'

I think the first one I got was a present from Kate Humble and came from a joke shop. The present model is not a joke. You fire it in the direction of the cat and it emits a sound like a model police car or ambulance. The cat usually turns and ambles away. It clearly doesn't find the noise unbearable at all. But I do.

Cat-scaring contraption number two is an electronic boxy thing that resembles a green version of the alarm you have at home so that you can hear if the baby is asleep. (Baby alarms rarely come in garden-friendly green.) This emits a sonic beam, or I assume it does as I can't hear it or see it. Neither can the cat when he walks past, until a little red light comes on which is presumably a clue. Supposedly, the sound of the sonic beam is unbearable to many cats, but not to this one. He doesn't look as if he's freaked out, he doesn't stick his paws in his ears, and more than once I have seen him sauntering towards the red light as if he wanted more volume, or to change the track.

I am not dissing any of these immaculately researched and scientifically proven products – some of them work, sometimes – and there are testimonies from cat owners, and for all I know from cats. Meanwhile, I have recently reverted to tried natural deterrents. It's rumoured that cats can't stand the whiff of orange or lemon peel. I put out whole reasonably fresh fruit, ready peeled, but my pied adversary took no notice. I had also read that cats can't abide elephant poo, either because they don't like the pong or because they think there are elephants loose in your garden, I don't know which. But in any case, before you can test it you first have to find your elephant poo. It's no good taking a bucket and a shovel to the local zoo, because elephants don't give rides and do mobile poos like in the olden days. Neither did I fancy trying to smuggle some through customs next time I go to Kenya. Clearly this is going to be a long battle. And I am not winning.

Only ten minutes ago I was taking my recommended five-minute break from computer cramp by gazing out of the window into the garden. The feeders were suspiciously empty, which is sure sign that devil cat was lurking, but I didn't realise how close. He was barely a few inches from the glass door. He was so totally absorbed in looking wicked and flexing his pouncing muscles, that at first he didn't notice me. He was transfixed by a pair of Goldfinches who had tinkled off to the safety of the top of our Silver Birch, and it was only when I turned the door key that he came out of his hunter's trance, looked up at me and gave me an insolent shrug – as if to say 'I am only looking' – before strolling away across the lawn at an intentionally provocative slow pace.

At that moment I recalled the ancient adage: 'If you can't beat 'em, join 'em.' I leapt into the garden, flapping and clapping, hissing, screeching, roaring, barking, and even adding a couple of meows. I even brandished my claws and shouted at him. 'Out. Out. *Out!*' He got the message. I really think he was genuinely panicked. He raced over the flowerbeds, nearly slipped into the frog pond, scrambled up the fence with so little control that he got momentarily stuck in the trellis (which amused me no end) and finally did a sort of feline Fosbury Flop over the top and dropped out of sight.

At that moment I was reminded of another adage: 'The old ways are the best.' Mind you, one thing is for certain: He'll be back. And so will I.

By the way… No cats were hurt in the writing of this chapter.

At this moment I am awaiting a consignment of Lion dung from an Internet supplier. It could go either way. It could scare the cat away, or make it dangerously randy.

Epilogue

A book like this is never really finished, in much the same way that a garden should never be considered complete. If I take a stroll past the front of other houses in the street where I live, there are some that of course change with the seasons, but they basically repeat themselves every year. They do it of their own accord, with little or no influence from whoever owns them, or from the man who is brought in to manicure the privet with a whining hedge trimmer, or to lop a few branches off the self-seeded sycamore with a high-decibel chain saw, both of which are pretty nasty noises, but not as obnoxious as the ghastly grating of the wretched leaf blower, which I'll swear they still use even when there is nothing to blow. Maybe in summer they bring their own bags of leaves and scatter them around so they have an excuse to brandish the blower. I suspect that some gardeners enjoy it because it looks rather like some kind of weapon from a violent computer game. Let's play 'World of Leafcraft' or 'Grand Theft Leaf-o.' The noise is certainly nastier than any laser gun I have ever heard.

Of course, we all have plants, trees, blossoms and flowers that we look forward to seeing each year at their appointed time. The front of a house belonging to one of our neighbours becomes totally festooned by a magnificent wisteria. Last year a pair of Jays nested in those crazy twisty branches, so close to the second-floor bay window that the householder could've stroked the nestlings. Blossoms and birds. Lovely. This spring I had a Blackcap singing in a magnolia. Very subtle. But for a truly novel colour combination I have to go for those pink birds with flashes of iridescent blue, framed by garlands of purple. It shouldn't work, but it certainly did, and I am delighted – and relieved – to say that never in twenty-odd years have I seen that Wisteria threatened by a pair of secateurs, let alone shears or an electric saw. Maybe the owner gives it a gentle yearly prune with the kitchen scissors, like granny trimming our lawn. What I have noticed is that he or she does not baulk at occasionally altering the layout of the garden. Flowers do come and go, as do various rocks, and just now and then an entertainingly incongruous 'object' appears. Most recently it was a very ancient metal mangle, which reminded me of my very first backyard in Rochdale. I immediately had a vision of my granny wringing out wet clothes over a big tin bath, which incidentally was also used as exactly that. A bath I mean. As a toddler I would get sponged down naked whilst standing in the tin bath on the kitchen table, visible through the window to anyone who passed by and was insensitive enough, or weird enough, to stare at me through the window. Not what I would call a fond memory, but enough to make me covet my neighbour's antique mangle. Especially now he's got a clematis curling round it. Just my style.

I must stop. This is exactly what happens when I go out and have a potter in my garden. I intend to spend no more than ten minutes and an hour later I am still there. This is usually because I have become absorbed in moving things around. That's why I understood Feng Shui Fox so well. There are, it has to be said, a lot of things that can be rearranged in my garden. A hundred gnomes for a start. Any new fake bird or animal gets tried in dozens of different locations and postures. I even spend ages placing pebbles along the edge of the lawn, constantly swapping them over until they are in the right order. What constitutes the 'right order' changes every time I go out there.

I decided to call this final chapter an 'Epilogue' and immediately winced and worried that maybe it sounded too much like an obituary. But then I thought, who knows? After all, there are worse places to be buried than in a garden. In fact I have already established a tradition of garden burials. There's a Woodpigeon that was clobbered by a Sparrowhawk, a frog which was a cat casualty, Limpy the Great Tit's deceased mate, and Toopee, a baby mouse that Laura had got very fond of. Toopee was a sad victim of me not checking the humane mousetrap often enough. He was so tiny I didn't realise he was in there. There is also a shady spot where Laura scattered her Auntie Joan's ashes alongside several model dinosaurs in what I call Jurassic Corner. No offence, Auntie Joan.

But enough of the past. What of the immediate future? First the not very good news. A new 'knock it down and start again' development has commenced upsettingly close to the back of our house. That should guarantee another year of hell. At least let's hope they get invaded by fleeing rats like we did.

I myself have a few resolutions. This will probably have to be the year that I finally break my sacred vow and 'get a man in.' I have to accept that the ravages of time have taken their toll on a variety of faculties, varying from the aggravating to the heartbreaking. Inevitably there are things I can no longer do, and some of them are in the garden. Like pollarding the willow tree which, although it was a mere sapling when I planted it, has grown so high that whoever goes up there will have to wear an oxygen mask and a parachute. Or do they get drones to do the high stuff now?

In any event I shall confine my activities and creativity to ground-level. I have started a project which I call 'natural sculptures.' I don't mean like an artist using natural materials. I don't do art. All I mean is that I shall keep a look out for large branches, sections of tree trunks and stumps that resemble animals or birds, real or imaginary. It is of course pretty silly, like a lot of what I do. My first centrepiece is called 'Loch Ness Monster swallowing a Hedgehog.' There will be more but please don't start sending me animal-shaped tree trunks and logs. If you find one why don't you have a go?

Talking of 'having a go,' I will conclude with a cheery positive little tale. Down at the bottom of our road, adjacent to the railway station, there is a little sliver of land, presumably too close to the train tracks on one side and the road on the other for it to ever be developed. This is in itself a rarity in the city. Little green spaces almost invariably eventually disappear under bricks and mortar. This hadn't happened to this little space, but on the other hand not much else had happened either. It was inevitably used as the local rubbish dump. Being so close to a station and the bus terminal meant that it was an irresistibly convenient place to chuck all the classic detritus of commuters, local workers and residents. Bottles, cartons and cans, discarded newspapers and the like.

However, the boss of an enterprising local business proposed not only a clean up, but also a transformation. It was to be called the World Peace Garden, which struck me as totally laudable, if perhaps a tad grandiose for a space barely twenty metres long.

I won't describe the whole process, or the outcome. Suffice it to say that it came to pass and it was good. Local people approved, supported and contributed time and effort. I myself can take no credit whatsoever. In fact, I have to confess that I barely noticed what was happening. However, when at last I made the short detour to have a proper perusal of the completed Peace Garden, I was not only delighted and impressed, but I felt considerable affinity with the 'style.' The main design and maintenance is overseen by an ingenious Cypriot guy. The phrase 'a man after my own heart' immediately sprang to mind. It was almost as if I was the apprentice coming face-to-face with the master. The flowers and plants flourish more spectacularly than will ever happen in my garden (not enough sun), but what I really related to was the meandering little paths, the natural wood seats and tables, the little ponds and marshy patches, and – my favourite features – archways and fencing all made from branches entwined in all kinds of totally natural yet slightly magical shapes. It is a great project, a great message and a great inspiration. Especially to me. Ever since then, I can be seen trudging back from the heath precariously balancing tree trunks and branches on my shoulder. Some will end up as wooden arches. Some will qualify to join the herd of natural sculptures.

And here's perhaps the best aspect. The garden has existed for two or three years now and it is forever changing and being changed. It is much used and much admired. Moreover, and this is so good to report, it has never been vandalised. Is that just Hampstead, or are people getting better?

Oops, sorry. One last thing… In case you were wondering, or even if you weren't, this is the checklist of species seen or heard in or over my present garden in North London. We have been here about 30 years.

Mute Swan	Lapwing	Magpie
Canada Goose	Oystercatcher	Jay
Mallard	Common Gull	Jackdaw
Shoveler	Black-headed Gull	Carrion Crow
Tufted Duck	Lesser Black-backed Gull	Goldcrest
Cormorant	Herring Gull	Blue Tit
Grey Heron	Common Tern	Great Tit
Great Crested Grebe	Feral Pigeon	Coal Tit
Red Kite	Woodpigeon	Skylark
Sparrowhawk	Stock Dove	Swallow
Common Buzzard	Collared Dove	House Martin
Honey Buzzard	Ring-necked Parakeet	Long-tailed Tit
Osprey	Tawny Owl	Common Whitethroat
Kestrel	Common Swift	Blackcap
Peregrine	Green Woodpecker	Chiffchaff
Hobby	Great Spotted Woodpecker	Willow Warbler

Nuthatch	Mistle Thrush	Chaffinch
Wren	Blackbird	Brambling
Starling	Robin	Greenfinch
Fieldfare	Dunnock	Goldfinch
Redwing	House Sparrow	Siskin
Song Thrush	Meadow Pipit	Lesser Redpoll

By the way, the Oystercatcher was flying over calling at night. I had just come back from Shetland, so maybe it followed me. If you weren't counting that comes to 66, Hopefully, if you were counting, it still comes to 66. I've never had a Treecreeper.

Other Natural History titles by Reed New Holland include:

1,000 Butterflies:
An Illustrated Guide to the Word's Most Beautiful Butterflies
Adrian Hoskins
ISBN 978 1 92151 756 5

Birds In Pictures
Markus Varesvuo
ISBN 978 1 92151 795 2

Birds: What's In A Name?
Peter Barry
ISBN 978 1 92554 604 0

Camouflaged Wildlife
Joe and Mary Ann McDonald
ISBN 978 1 92151 786 0

Deadly Oceans
Nick and Caroline Robertson-Brown
ISBN 978 1 92151 782 2

Field Guide to Mushrooms of Britain and Europe
Alison Linton
ISBN 978 1 92151 773 0

Field Guide to Trees of Britain and Europe
Alan Birkett
ISBN 978 1 92151 783 9

Freshwater Fishes of Britain
Jack Perks
ISBN 978 1 92151 777 8

Great British Birding Experiences
Dan Brown
ISBN 978 1 92151 775 4

Owls of the World
James Duncan
ISBN 978 1 92151 764 8

Nature's Greatest Migrations
Marianne Taylor
ISBN 978 1 92151 785 3

Raptors In Focus:
A Quest to find Birds of Prey in Europe and beyond
Dick Forsman
ISBN 978 1 92151 768 6

Seabirds of the World
David Tipling
ISBN 978 1 92151 767 9

Top Wildlife Sites of the World
Will and Natalie Burrard-Lucas
ISBN 978 1 92151 759 4

Volcano Discoveries
Tom Pfeiffer and Ingrid Smet
ISBN 978 1 92151 735 8

Wildlife On Your Doorstep
Mark Ward
ISBN 978 1 92151 774 7

For details of these and hundreds of other Natural History titles see www.newhollandpublishers.com

First published in 2017 by Reed New Holland Publishers Pty Ltd
London • Sydney • Auckland

The Chandlery, 50 Westminster Bridge Road, London SE1 7QY, UK
1/66 Gibbes Street, Chatswood, NSW 2067, Australia
5/39 Woodside Avenue, Northcote, Auckland 0627, New Zealand

www.newhollandpublishers.com

A record of this book is held at the British Library and the
National Library of Australia.

ISBN 978 1 92151 778 5

Group Managing Director: Fiona Schultz
Publisher and Project Editor: Simon Papps
Designer: Andrew Davies
Production Director: James Mills-Hicks
Printer: Times Offset Malaysia Sdn Bhd

10 9 8 7 6 5 4 3 2 1

Keep up with New Holland Publishers on Facebook
www.facebook.com/NewHollandPublishers